INTRODUC

On the floor of my office "vaults" re͟s͟ ͟
stuffed to overflowing with literally thousan͟u͟s͟ ͟
horoscopes, each hiding its own fascinating story[1]!
Although I've written several books of interest to serious
students and professionals alike, it is now time to share
my "hands on" experience with the public.

Astrologers need new words to best describe our work
to a culture that knows so little about what professional
astrologers really do. The colorful word-concept
"Astrology" is all too laden with fantasy, glamour
misconceptions and prejudice.

Frankly, the practice of Astrology is more accurately
described as Cosmobiology, the actual name of a
distinctive school within our field. Another helpful term
might be Astral Mechanics; whereas the birth chart or
"horoscope" might more aptly be termed the Astral
Schematic, (a word coined by by coauthor Andrea
Gehrz.)

Now let's start all over again.

"Hello, I'm a Cosmos Biologist.

May I welcome you to the fascinating and useful
world of Cosmos Biology?"

---

[1] Other names for the horoscope used in these stories are:
planetary birth map, natal chart, birth chart, or birth map.

Different, right? One can instantly feel how these new words clear the palate of the mind, allowing us to better receive a fresh understanding of our field.

You see, the true and profound study of Astrology is not all that different from studying the effects of the weather on mood, health, finance or vegetables.

The Planetary Birth Chart caste for the minute of a person's birth truly is a telescope into that human being on all levels: spiritually, psychologically, vocationally, and physically. Astrology is also an useful window into the larger rhythms of nature, being able to assist us with weather patterns, planting the garden, politics, selecting surgery dates, stock trading, seismology, etc. There exists no study that is parallel in scope to Astrology!

Astrology is preeminently a science which seeks to define and describe the quality of time, and thus the implication of changing vibrational patterns upon the Earth and her inhabitants: physically, mentally, emotionally, spiritually.

Perhaps this is why some (not all!) scientists deny its validity. For decades, modern "science" has accepted only a quantitative measure of time as valuable or even real. In other words, we have been measuring seconds, hours and light years of time, while denying the fact that time also carries within it a certain mood!

Recent discoveries are changing this lopsided paradigm, as we have witnessed the arrival of Chrono-medicine, a new medical model that stresses the effects of solar-lunar cycles in the timing of medical treatment. Personally, I've known several PHD scientists who also have taken up a serious study of Astrology. As Bob Dylan's famous folk song goes, "the times they are a'changing."

And indeed this is true, as time is constantly changing! It is important to notice that each moment of time has its own distinct quality. Each day or hour is infused with a certain color, a tone, a flavor. This can also be thought of in the practical sense. One day is best for brewing beer, while another favors planting roses.

Our curiously American cultural prejudice against the knowledge of solar and lunar effects has produced some undesirable results. For instance, doctors continue to conduct surgeries under the effects of full moons and eclipses, although it has been common knowledge for millennia that these lunar-based time periods can create complications such as hemorrhaging. If the Moon swells the tides, wouldn't she also pull on that blood that flows within us? Much of the truth behind Astrology's profound workings can be explained through pure common sense! It is unfortunate that such great wisdom is shunned in today's halls of medicine and science.

This was not always the case. Prior to 1666, European physicians needed to pass their astrological exams in order to become licensed. Blagreve's Physic, which is the diary of a Renaissance doctor, aptly displays the high level of astrological skill that has been historically required of the Greek, Medieval and Renaissance doctors. Professional astrologers patiently await the day when this old knowledge is brought back in order to save many lives!

It is also interesting to conceive of the fact that spatial direction also holds within it a certain feeling or quality. The ancients discovered that the twelve directions exert varying influences. For instance, the infrared in-fluxing of planets positioned to the north of us is quite different than planets that are posited south of us. Planets to the north have a unique quality as they are being shielded by the body of the earth, while planets to the south can be felt shining boldly overhead!

The twelve directional positions of the planets in the sky around us provide the astrologer with a wealth of interpretive meaning. These celestial directions comprise the traditional twelve astrological "houses." Since ancient times these twelve houses have described the stage and focus of daily life activities: i.e. home, children, career, marriage, etc. These twelve directions also may reveal the deepest spiritual and psychological information.

As the Sun journeys along the great belt of the ecliptic, it bathes the Earth in twelve vibrations, depending on its seasonal position within its yearly cyclic relationship to our Earth. These twelve "vibrations" might be better thought of as twelve moods, also known as the twelve zodiac signs! Each sign is a season, infused with, and expressing in its "natives" an intrinsic quality and experience on many levels of their being.

A Wonderbook of
True Astrological Case Files

Judith Hill
Andrea Gehrz

STELLIUM
PRESS

ISBN 978-0-9827893-3-9

Stellium Press

MOIRA + STELLIUM =

dedicated to the resurrection, continuance and
expansion of ancient knowledge

CONTENTS

TRUE STORIES ✿ JUDITH HILL

TRUE STORIES ✌ ANDREA L. GEHRZ

For Dad

Critics cite that some astrologers use a "wrong zodiac" because the constellations have precessed backwards over time; failing to realize that we aren't using a star based zodiac at all! Rather, we use twelve seasons, with our sign cycle commencing upon the Spring Equinox, an Earth-Sun angular relationship that remains the same today as it was ten million years ago!

The first day of the sign "Aries" occurs on the Spring Equinox, irregardless of the position of the constellation sign of "Aries" overhead. In our system, an "Aries" person is born between zero-thirty days after the Spring Equinox. Please understand that "Sign" has two meanings, thus causing our critic's misunderstanding! The word "sign" can refer either to a constellation of stars, or to an earthly season. These are not the same thing! Seasonally based "tropical" astrologers are also well aware of the stars above and use them for select purposes. However, the constellations don't reflect the basis for our Earth-Sun based sign cycle.

Each of the twelve earthly seasons (signs) belongs to one of four elements and also to one of three modes. The four astrological elements represent <u>four levels of density in matter</u>: fire, air, water, earth. The three astrological modes, indicate the <u>rate of matter in motion:</u> cardinal, fixed and mutable. The four elements and the three modes combine in a perfect mathematical equation of:

4 elements x 3 modes = 12 signs

Aries = Fire, Cardinal   Libra = Air, Cardinal

Taurus = Earth, Fixed
Gemini = Air, Mutable
Cancer = Water, Cardinal
Leo = Fire, Fixed
Virgo = Earth, Mutable

Scorpio = Water, Fixed
Sagittarius = Fire, Mutable
Capricorn = Earth, Cardinal
Aquarius = Air, Fixed
Pisces = Water, Mutable

Each sign expresses a special quality, created by a unique wedding of vibrational density (the element of that sign) and rate of motion (the mode of that sign).

The solar system and the stars can also be seen to function as a giant clock. As the planets wander along the vault of stars, they stir and impart upon us a magnificent sea of endlessly changing space-time vibrational combinations. We as incarnated beings are thus fashioned from this celestial fabric, having been imprinted by the cosmos upon our very first breath! No other person is created exactly like us. And neither can the unique atmosphere imbuing our birth moment ever be repeated.

We Cosmos-biologists do not know entirely how this celestial imprinting actually occurs, but we do observe its obvious results, (as demonstrated in the upcoming stories). And we are also sure that the chart influences the experience throughout the entirety of the current lifetime.

At the risk of demystifying Astrology, it is high time that we discuss what Astrology is not.

Astrology is not: an occult art; a religion; a psychic science. Neither is Astrology an exclusive nor mandatory predictive tool.

Let us elucidate upon these four points.

There is nothing any more "occult" about purely practiced Astrology than there is behind the practice of making music, studying chemistry, predicting the weather, or even the study of radio signals. It is entirely possible to study the effects of the solar system upon us in much the same way as we study the effects of sound waves, the fluctuations of magnetic fields, nutrition or even solar storms. The purist astrologer is doing exactly these things.

An astrologer is a weatherman who studies the effects of the astral weather. Sure, an astrologer might also choose to be an occultist, but so might also your doctor, or even the neighborhood plumber! The practice and knowledge of Astrology does not demand nor rest upon occultism, nor any other world view, but instead it relies upon observation.

It is curious to note for instance that most of our Western astrological mapping systems were developed by Christian monks. If astrologers are universally occultists, then so are all scientists who study the fluctuations of hidden energies and their effects upon human beings.

Astrology is not a religion. Amongst the ranks of the historically great astrologers we find devout Christians,

Jews, Buddhists, Muslims, Hindus and Pagans. We also find the occasional Atheist or Agnostic. Astrology is at once an art and a science, and like its estranged brother Astronomy, the field of Cosmos-biology itself is not the province of any one faith.

Astrology is not intrinsically a psychic art. Astrologers can interpret planetary patterns without utilizing their psychic faculties. Certainly psychic insight is useful to all consulting professions, but the use of psychism is not required of practicing astrologers. No doubt certain persons of intuitive temperament become astrologers. Psychically sensitive persons might also be drawn to psychology, music, healing, religion, poetry, etc. In essence, Astrology is not a "psychic science" though nothing prevents its use as a psychic tool!

Astrology at its most basic level could be said to be a knowledge of the cosmic energies as they interact with humanity throughout space and time. The study and use of Astrology for practical and useful purposes could more accurately be termed "Astral Mechanics."

The predictive branches of Astrology, (forbidden by some Christian groups)[2], are not actually "predicting" future events in the biblical sense at all, because the predicted outcomes are rarely seen as immutable. So what is the forecasting astrologer doing? He/She is

---

[2] despite the King James version of Genesis 1:14, Matthew 2:2, Matthew 2:7 and many other potentially if not obvious pro-Astrology statements about the use of the planets and stars as prophetic signs.

making an assessment of planetary energetics and is attempting to determine how these unseen forces might influence a person, farm or nation. This assessment strategy is nearly identical to that used by other predictive professions, e.g. weathermen, seismologists, doctors, or cycles analysts.

Oddly, these professions find no objection with the same groups that decry Astrology as "unholy work." Those concerned should understand that the more prophetic uses of Astrology comprise a small percent of an astrologer's true work, and are optional. For instance, vocational, natal, psychological, agricultural and medical uses of Astrology involve no prediction unless one chooses to analyze the future planetary "weather" related to these specific topics.

Truly, it is amazing to comprehend the sheer number of highly practical uses for the planetary birth chart! In any given week, I might as a professional astrologer be hired to select the best employees for a shoe store or find the best date to open an ice cream shop. My work week can be quite interesting and varied, as I spend my time planning the best routes for a vacation, choosing between three prospective realtors, or selecting the safest date for surgery. I routinely suggest careers to my clients; have consulted with chefs on upcoming food fads, and have even provided the best times for a llama to conceive a desirable female offspring. I have traced seismological activity, found a lost dog, compared Minnesota with Japan, and assisted psychiatrists with inexplicable mental disorders.

The great American prophet and devout Christian Edgar Cayce was asked:

"Is it proper for us to study the effects of the planets upon our lives, in order to understand our tendencies and inclinations better, as they are influenced by the planets?"

Cayce's answer was a powerful yes, with a caveat.
"It is proper to study Astrology when it is studied aright, as it is very, very, very much worth while. Then how is it studied aright? By studying the influence (of the planets) in the light of knowledge already obtained by mortal man. Give out more of that knowledge - giving the understanding that the will must ever be the guiding factor leading a man on and ever upward."

The best astrologers are spiritually grounded, widely read, and proficient scholars in many fields. A good practicing astrologer should have a vast understanding of humanity, as this will enable the astrologer to tackle a wide variety of client concerns.

My own science background has also enabled me to understand the skeptic. Why? Because I am a skeptic too! Years of statistical research and personal chart work have satisfied my skeptical inclinations by proving that Astrology works. Nowadays, I am more curious to discover HOW it works.

Personally, I've invested ten years into the statistical research of both astro-genetic and astro-seismic phenomena. My own testimony for Astrology's validity has been based not on belief, but instead upon a considerable amount of statistical work, and also upon the completion of approximately nine thousand personal astrological chart readings with clients. This factually-created knowing within me that Astrology does work encouraged me to accept and participate in a skeptic's challenge, sponsored through the National Council of Geocosmic Research. During this challenge, three astrologers (myself included) correctly matched up five astrological charts with five biographies, and we have the newspaper report to prove it!

There is currently a growing contingent of card carrying scientists who are avid students and researchers of Astrology. I've personally known several! Although it is apparent that a new day has dawned, the renegade affection of brilliant minds for Astrology is not new. Johannes Kepler, Tycho Brahe, George Washington, Arthur Young and Carl Jung were all skilled practitioners of Astrology, as were (and are) many other geniuses of note. Moreover, there are at least two groups devoted to the research and advancement of Astrology; the National Council for Geocosmic Research (NCGR) and the Institute for the Study and Advancement of Astrological Research (ISAAR). And thus, we cannot claim that there is no scientific research in existence to support and affirm the mysterious influence of the planets upon earth life.

Scientists now recognize entanglement theory. According to entanglement theory, two atoms briefly bonded together, when untangled, will continue to vibrate with one another no matter how far they are separated. Even at one million miles apart, two previously-bonded atoms do still communicate! The reason why this happens is not yet known. Without realizing it, scientists have offered an explanation for the planetary effects that seem to happen upon humans at a distance.

Entanglement Theory itself disempowers the tired "scientific" argument that the planets cannot possibly affect us because their gravitational pull is less than that of a passing bus! It could be said that during the moment of our first breath, we somehow entangle for life with the atomic structure of the solar system as it is configured at the minute we enliven.

While entanglement theory may not entirely explain the mechanism behind the uncanny workings of Astrology, it now joins the ranks of many extant theories. New insights are emerging from many quarters to explain the mechanism behind Cosmos-biology. These recent theories might someday explain the efficacy and accuracy of the astrological chart.

Physicist Buryl Payne has developed new hypotheses for planetary influence as transferred through magnetic fields and atmospheric water molecules. While the intent of his work is not distinctly astrological, his findings open a scientific discussion regarding planetary and seasonal influences upon Earthlings. He states:
"...it has been discovered that Earth has a highly variable magnetic field and is radiated continuously and variably by the Sun with streams of electrons and photons and other

particles called 'the solar wind'. Observations have shown that both the Sun's activity and the variations of the Earth's magnetic field are altered by the positions of the planets. This provides a physical mechanism which links the planets to events on earth. I have observed links with some weather patterns, human personal behavior, and human mass behavior." Payne has further comments that these planet induced fluctuations of the earth's magnetic field affect our brain rhythms, and glandular balances.

Pioneering scientists of Payne's calibre are too few, and still encounter significant prejudice within the their scientific communities. However, their remarkable work will seed a future understanding of the "why" and "how" of astrological influence.

It is our hope that the discoveries of the ancient scientists will be understood in the new light of certain modern revelations. It is both Andrea's experience and mine that there is no tool of greater value than Astrology in reference to its ability to see into a human being on all levels; spiritually, psychologically, vocationally, and physically. In anticipation of the day when our philosophical and deep science of Astrology is recognized for its great gifts to humanity, we gladly present;

A Wonderbook of True Astrological Case Files

"And God said, let there be lights in the firmament of the heaven to divide the day from the night; and let them be for signs, and for seasons, for days, and years."

King James   Genesis 1:14

Preface

On a recent foray to the Portland Main Library downtown, I discovered the profession of "Astrologer" to be listed in both giant vocational guides under the erroneous heading of "Entertainer." Lamentably, our divine mother of sciences was catalogued twice under this wildly inaccurate rubric! How the once sacred science of Astrology fell from its revered podium is another story all its own. For our purposes here, it is enough to say that until the late seventeenth century, every physician was required to attain a high level of proficiency in the skill of Astrology before attaining his medical license. The once revered position of our field might very well be acknowledged with a question about the Bible.

Just who were the three "Magi" anyway?

Obviously, until fairly recent times, Astrology held high status as one of mankind's greatest and most useful of studies.

Pondering my library's ignorant classification of Astrology, I wanted to help correct this collective misconception. It seemed as though a public education program was in order. But then, how could one educate a public that knows nothing of the real nature of the science of Astrology, much less its true uses and purpose?

My years spent in the statistical examination of Astrology have indeed produced astonishing results, but this research has yet to make a tiny dent in the wall of prejudice that still prevails against the astral sciences. What could be done?

One fine day, it finally occurred to me that we all love stories, and here I was sitting on a gold mine of real case files! Within these pages exists a whole book of them. The amazing stories in this volume present to the reader an intimate window into the breadth and depth of genuine Astrology as it is practiced by sincere and highly trained professionals. By reading these stories about the use and function of Astrology, the reader will absorb certain truths about this time honored astral science.

Within the stories that follow, I have altered names and other personal details in order to protect the identity of those mentioned. The details of each case are exactly true to life, as I can best remember them. Permissions have been obtained where feasible.

This collection comprises a mere sampling of the vast array of astonishing incidences recalled from a lifetime of astrological case work with everything from horses to houses! Most of these cases are decades old, and some of the players herein may no longer be with us. I have cherry picked these cases not so much as to 'wow' the reader, but rather to enlighten the reader about the use and function of Astrology.

It is surely true that there exist more impressive cases than these, such as the time I submitted in writing the exact week and details of the coming disaster at Chernobyl, to the Oakland Tribune! Or the time that I warned my investing clients about the upcoming August 2008 stock market crash. Nor have I included the full account of how three astrologers (including myself) accepted the aforementioned skeptic's challenge and won by correctly matching five horoscopes to five brief biographies.

Although bemused by these "feats," I've regarded them as the natural fruit of disciplined experience. All decent astrologers undoubtedly have similar portfolios of their best work. The following true stories of astrological prowess are really no different than examples of mastery in any other craft, e.g. juggling, cooking, or predicting the weather.

The point of sharing these stunning case files is not to boast of marvels although the profound accuracy of Astrology is in fact a magnificent truth. Successes such as these should seem normal to any solid and accomplished practitioner of the cosmobiological arts.

I have written down these fascinating cases for several reasons. First of all, these stories are a testament to the fact that certain qualified and skilled astrologers do exist. Most essentially, these stories serve to educate the reader about our field, and in doing so, shift these persistently errant stereotypes that dominate the American mindset regarding Astrology and its practitioners. And lastly, we have written this Wonderbook book for our reader's personal delight.

The stories herein are representative of the everyday concerns that find their way into an astrologer's case load. Both amusing and tragic, they run the gamut of human experience, while offering the reader a window into what astrologers really do in the course of a day's work.

Cases were selected to enable our reader to discover for him/herself what Astrology really is, and something of its traditional applications. The open-minded reader will find the upcoming true cases to be an entertaining way to discover the mysteries of this marvelous science.

These stories offer the reader far more than a remarkable read. Each case stimulates at least one of the greater questions of life. One cannot practice the celestial arts without wrestling with the great spiritual questions of: free will, destiny, grace, fate, karma and character.

To describe the quality of time, to relieve suffering, and to help shed light upon those practical conundrums of everyday life - this is the true work of the astrologer. And ever so much more! Truly, no telescope exists as multifaceted and wondrous as the astrological birth chart.

My co-author Andrea's stories provide a second testimony into the astonishing usefulness of the most excellent art of Astrology.

We have thoroughly enjoyed collaborating on this book!

May you the reader enjoy the fruits of our labor as much as we have. With great joy, we offer this little treasure trove of true stories to those minds and hearts whom wish to receive it.

True Stories

Judith Hill

PERFECT FAITH

I've had all kinds of clients. But nobody like Gabrielle. A strong, buxom woman, Gabrielle strode with exceptional poise into my tiny office, confidently proclaiming:

"You are a Vocational Astrologer. Therefore, you should be able to guess what it is that I do for work!"

She removed her purple suede coat and sat down, placing her diamond festooned hand firmly upon the green silk table cloth.

Please understand that playing "test-the-astrologer" games is not my favorite activity. I prefer reading charts for folks who desire to reap the benefits of this remarkable ancient knowledge. Nevertheless, something about Gabrielle's strident challenge intrigued me. She explained that she had many successful years under her belt doing exactly what she was born to do, and therefore, I should be able to precisely describe what it was she does for a living.

Gabrielle's chart was fascinating! Almost all her planets were clustered in one corner of the circular chart, creating for her an intense life focus that we astrologers know as a "stellium". This beautiful old Latin word means: *"A place where the stars stand together"*; and refers to a chart condition wherein five or more planets are standing all together in one sign.

Pondering Gabrielle's chart, I realized that this rare *stellium* configuration must be the key to our career guessing-game challenge! This planetary cluster was happily situated in Leo the Lion, the sign of kings. Leo is a natural boss who also likes sports and other entertaining events. The sign of Leo also rules managers. Next, I checked her stellium's direction. The planets were tightly grouped in the southeast direction of the heavens at the moment of Gabrielle's birth.

The southeastern sky is better known to astrologers as "the eleventh house." This celestial direction in the chart is associated with large groups of all kinds.

"Ok" I ventured, *"Maybe you manage athletics teams...or large entertainment groups."*

Gabrielle appeared nonplussed. She proudly agreed,

"Yes, I am the Manager of the _____ Sports Team."

Of course, I cannot reveal the name of this famous athletic team, but it was all the riot at the time! Curiously, Gabrielle showed no surprise whatever at her birth chart's astonishing accuracy. It appeared as if she completely expected me to accomplish this feat in the same manner she might have expected her hair dresser to guess her true hair color. Gabrielle appeared to have had a perfect faith in Astrology. I was myself impressed with the typical yet amazing accuracy of the astrological chart, but kept this thought a secret only to myself.

DON'T BE SUPERSTITIOUS!

"Please come on Friday," she said, *"it is more convenient."*

Bonnie, a dear friend from my Berkeley days, asked me to visit her ranch in the hauntingly beautiful oak hills of northern California. However, I was worried.

"My ephemeris of planetary positions alerts us that this Friday is a most inauspicious date for plane travel. Please allow me to arrive on Saturday instead!"

Bonnie rankled. *"Don't be so superstitious!"* she replied. This rude retort surprised me, as Bonnie was a longtime client and an enthusiastic recipient of my books. I held my ground.

"No, I will come Saturday because Friday looks like an extremely poor choice for air travel."

It was true. The planetary alignments showed "foul weather" for that Friday's airline departures over Portland, Oregon. Bonnie relented, but was not pleased.

Friday came around, and to everyone's astonishment, the Portland airport was closed because of a fraudulent bomb scare. Absolutely no departures were permitted!

However, on Saturday, I flew out with ease under perfect skies, in more ways than one. Bonnie never said another word about the incident, and she never again called me *superstitious* either.

MY BUS RIDE

You are probably aware of the fact that there are twelve signs of the zodiac. You might even know your own birth sign, and perhaps, something of its character. But, did you know that every single one of the 365 days of the year carries a certain unique "feeling" as well?

This concept makes quite a bit of sense if you think about it. The scientists tell us that we are made out of light particles that are supplied to us by the Sun. Scientists call these light particles *photons*. This is a fancy way of saying that we are made out of sunlight.

Each birth day is unique to any other day of the year! Why? Because each day our earth receives a slightly different slant of solar light beams as she journeys through the seasonal circle of the year. To those attuned to subtle moods, the special "feel" of each day is a palpable experience!

We astrologers call these 365 days of the yearly Earth-Sun dance the *"360 degrees of Celestial Longitude."* (This number obviously varies from the 365 days of our typical calendar year.) I've included this wonderful little true tale because it so aptly demonstrates this uniqueness of each day of the year.

One drippy Portland day circa 1989, I boarded the 15 Belmont bus heading downtown. In those less populated days some bus drivers were unusually friendly, and so it was not uncommon for a bored driver to engage a rider in patter should one sit nearby. On this particular day, the bus was empty as I took my usual seat up front near the driver. He immediately struck up a lively conversation, and we chatted freely as the bus moved along its route. Somehow the discussion got around to what it is that I do for a living, and the conversation verged onto Astrology.

 "I know a bit about Astrology myself!" remarked the burly bus driver, who commenced an entertaining dialogue about what was clearly his keen interest. We bumped along through traffic, discussing the finer points of the Moon.

Soon it was time for me to exit the bus, and I rang the bell. *"Next stop, please."*

I stood up and prepared to disembark, clutching the cold overhead balance bar. The bus stopped and the door gasped open *"pshhhhhhhawww."* I looked back. The bus driver was studying me with a mischievous eye.

"Your Moon is at 15 degrees of Sagittarius!" he stated with an unflinching certainty. And he was perfectly right[3]!

Imagine my surprise. One shot in 360 degrees and he announces the precise celestial degree of my birth Moon's position with as much confidence as if he was calling out the next street name.

---

[3] this degree is a stand-in for the author's actual Moon degree at birth

This was no mere coincidence, as the bus driver had never seen my actual birth chart. We hadn't met before, nor exchanged names, and thus he did not know me nor did I know him. My photograph was unpublished and my profile low. Stranger still, few folks discuss Moon signs. The Sun sign is far more popular! Most of my friends don't even know my Moon sign, much less its exact degree.

Although weird or even "impossible" seeming, this is not the first time that this sort of thing has happened, and nor will it be the last. The unique quality and mood of each day's year is as obvious to the gifted observer as own nose. In more specific terms, it could be said that the most sensitive of bus drivers can sometimes put the ball in the hoop by guessing the exact zodiacal degree upon which a person was born. Or better still, the precise position of their birth Moon.

Maybe the scientists should make a study of *that!*

THE LIFE GUARD

"Keep your wife near you at all times!" I strictly urged.

"During the whole time period of your maritime vacation, never allow her to be far from your sight!"

Dermot and Gail Donnelly were a delightful couple in their mid-fifties. They were also two of my favorite clients, having used my services for everything from real estate listing times to vocational insights. Gail was a small, wise and cheerful woman ~~that I especially~~ especially enjoyed. Dermot was a wild artist wh~~o worked~~ as a day job beaurocrat. Today, they sat in my ~~office~~ revealing their vacation plans to the Bahamas. Their charts were placed before me, ready for inspection.

As I examined Dermot's chart, I noticed something quite amiss. Neptune, the old Greek God of the oceans was sitting exactly over Dermot's *South Lunar Node*, a horoscopic point that has historically been associated with drowning. Simultaneously, the current *South Lunar Node* was parked exactly over Dermot's' own birth placement of Neptune! This compounded influence indicated double trouble from our dear friend Neptune, and certainly warned of danger from the sea.

I said, *"Dermot, your chart warns you not to swim. Do not go into the ocean, do not sail or snorkel. Frankly, it might be wise to avoid hot tubs. However, whatever you do, keep your wife near you at all times! She will protect you."*

"Why is that?" asked Gail, perhaps not particularly keen on being her husband's constant body guard.

"Gail," I said, *"When you were born, Jupiter, the planet of protectors, represented you, and was simultaneously sitting exactly on Dermot's rising sign degree, a horoscopic point which represents him. You are clearly his great protector!"*

Gail listened attentively, but said nothing more about it. Naturally, the Donnellys ignored my consternations. Immediately upon arriving in the Bahamas, the happy couple donned snorkeling gear and dived off into the warm and inviting sea.

As Gail related the story to me upon their return, the two were paddling about the reefs when Dermot vanished. Looking around she could see him nowhere! She dived beneath the surface only to find Dermot already unconscious, who having drowned was now floating limply in the current. Gail hoisted Dermot's body up from the briny depths, hauled him to shore, and resuscitated him. He miraculously survived and continues on doing many good works to this very day.

> *Dermot's astrologically appointed body guard had saved his life!*

You see, unbeknownst to me at the time of their reading, his wife Gail was once a trained lifeguard.

PRIMO MOBILE XXXXVIIII 49

WRONG STATION

David knocked on the door and walked in. He was a thin, attractive man, casually-attired with refined features, a high forehead and wispy light hair. David projected an air of thoughtful intelligence and genuine goodwill.

"Oh Oh," I said, *"I think we must have the wrong birth time on your chart."*

"No" He insisted,*" I am absolutely certain that I was born at noon. There is no doubt."*

I couldn't disagree more!

"It is not possible you were born at noon," I replied, noting that his "rising sign" didn't fit him at all.

"You don't look like a Pisces rising. You don't dress like a Pisces rising, or talk like one, and you certainly don't vibrate like one! You MUST have had Aquarius rising at birth, and this would have been two hours earlier, at least."

The "rising sign" is the special sign that is rising up on the eastern horizon at the very moment that a person is being born. In certain ways we do not yet understand, this sign sets up our life's cyclic pattern and the general tone of the world at the moment when we are busy taking our very first and independent breath.

Now you must be wondering just how I might have known that David was not born at noon, but instead near 10 a.m. The answer to this question lies in the fact that people *look* like their charts just as much as they look like their parents. Sometimes more!

And yes, each of the twelve rising signs has its own "look" and feel, though its not quite all that simple. Most of us look like a blend of our strongest horoscopic components.

The study of what people look like according to their astrological charts is called "astro-physiognomy." My early obsession with this subject led to the publication of *The Astrological Body Types*. The pages of this book are copiously illustrated with the traditional astrological sign, planetary and elemental types. Often, this knowledge comes in extremely handy, and the day I met David was one of those times!

No matter how much I tried to convince him of his Aquarius rising, David would not agree with my assessment, remaining adamant that I complete a reading for what any seasoned astrologer could plainly see was an inaccurate birth time.

"I just know you are born at 10 a.m.," I said, continuing what turned out to be a curiously mismatched reading. Everything seemed wrong, and I could not "get" the right information from the chart. It was as though my antenna could not pick up David's radio signal, because I was not tuned in to the correct radio station.

This is no mystery. If our cell phones are programed with unique codes enabling us to "reach" our calling party, then why shouldn't David's correct birth time, as mirrored by his natal chart, allow me to reach his specific frequency?

David thought so too. *"This reading doesn't seem to fit me at all!"* He complained as he left my office disappointed with what appeared to be an "off" reading. Nevertheless, he remained unbending that the noon birth time he gave me was correct.

(I noted to myself that David's stubbornness was further proof of an Aquarius rising sign.)

Some weeks later, I received a call from David.

"You were right after all!" he exclaimed. *"I found an old birth record in a my baby book, and sure enough, I was born at 10 a.m.!"*

From that moment forward, David's horoscope fit him like a comfortable shoe and "worked." Once I had the right chart in hand, I could pick up its signals just fine. The vibrations broadcasting from his personal "radio station" had cleared.

THE SULLEN TEEN

Heinrich proudly dropped off his attractive nineteen year old daughter Robyn for her first natal reading. However, it soon became strikingly clear that this endeavor was not this girl's idea of a good time!

Robyn parked herself in my beautifully carved teak client chair and crossed her arms.

Although an attractive brunette, Robyn refused to evince any facial expression other than sullen resignation. It was clear that she didn't want to "give away" any information about herself, and was either playing "test the astrologer," or would tolerate what she preconceived to be ninety minutes of nonsense in order to please her father. I began Robyn's reading, describing her talents, strengths, weaknesses, and general character as indicated in her astrological chart.

"Your planetary birth chart shows outstanding testimonies of a high degree of athletic prowess."

"Nope," she said. *"That's not me."*

I was flummoxed. The great majority of "testimonies" in the chart all pointed to sports.

Sports, sports, sports!

"Well, you must not have discovered this about yourself yet," I went on. *"Sometimes we have a talent that lies latent within us, much like a sleeping volcano."*

Robyn pondered this idea as though it was an unexpected insect in her soup.

"You could be an Olympian." I continued. *"Are you sure you have no special gift in athletics?"*

"I don't think so," she curtly replied, *"nothing special,"* continuing to stare straight ahead. Robyn sat there stiffly, refusing to engage. I couldn't fathom her denials because so many planetary testimonies in her birth chart suggested a fine athlete!

For the remainder of her reading I floundered about, wondering if I had been given the wrong birth time. Fathers have been known to give me imperfect data, even wrong years!

Truly, there are few things I dislike worse than reading charts for someone who doesn't wish to be there. This can feel a bit like being silently mocked while doing one's job. Robyn's reading ended precisely when her father knocked on the door. He arrived as cheerfully as he had departed. The impassive Robyn stood next to him. *"You like your reading honey?"* he beamed. She grunted, refusing to lose the impassive mug.

"I'm so proud of her! Did you know that at fifteen she was the number 1 rated basketball player in the state?"

Oh oh, Robyn was busted. However, she remained as stoic as ever.

Two years later I received a call from her Dad. Robyn had landed a top job at a much coveted athletics firm. According to her chart, this is an excellent career choice! We can readily predict that Robyn will bat home runs in her new arena of sports business.

MY ASTRO TWIN

One would think that a good way to discover if Astrology "works" is to find that special someone who was also born exactly when you were; meaning that they were born at the exact same time, place, day and year as you. This person could very simply be described as your "astro-twin!"

Make no mistake, each created being most likely has a number of *astro-twins*, as there are babies, butterflies, bears and many other beings sharing any given birth moment.

So what does the horoscope show us anyway?

A person's Planetary Birth Chart reveals the unique set of inborn tendencies and unfolding life circumstances to be used and experienced in this very lifetime. The innate capacities and character of an incoming spirit are shown in the natal chart through a type of code. This approach assumes the existence of a spirit that is born into a body. Although we share a set of life circumstances and traits with an astro-twin, our spirits remain eternally separate and unique. Therefore, two people may share a birth chart, but this doesn't guarantee that they will be at all alike.

Or does it? One way to study this question is to compare the lives of *astro-twins,* who are two persons that share the same birth chart.

I didn't set out to find my astro-twin. She found me, by accident.

One fine day as I was opening the data slips sent in by the public to *The Redhead's Research Project* (we were studying the positions of Mars in naturally redheaded people), my attention stood still. There in my hand was a slip inscribed by a woman sharing my day, year and time! She was born just five minutes earlier, in a nearby town. The charts were nearly identical.

Who was this lady, and what did she do?

It turns out this woman was a distinguished lifetime professional astrologer, and a redhead to boot. She and I also shared the same ethnic background. To top it off, she is a long time professional performer (music and drama), whereas I have a side "hobby" profession as a performing musician and have recorded as a house musician on several albums. There were numerous other profound if not weird similarities, too personal to detail here. To tell you the truth, even I was stunned by these correlations. But, let's be skeptical. Could our profound similarities be only mere coincidence?

Ok, what are the chances here? Please understand here that there are (at most) a few hundred persons in the United States that are life time professional consulting astrologers. And the Jewish population stands at about 2% worldwide (there are more Buddhists in the United States than Jews).

Performing musicians, while far more common than full time astrologers, are also rare. We must ask ourselves; what do our numbers indicate here?

In the world, just how many known, lifetime professional astrologers exist that are also Jewish, red or auburn haired and sideline in the performance arts? In a world population of six billion, I would offer the figure would stand at five, if we are lucky, and I've never yet heard of any others. One thing we do know for sure is that two of them are *astro-twins*!

DOG TALES

You might have heard of "the Dog Star" Sirius. There is also a dog's planet, which is the planet of Mars. That's right. Mars represents dogs, or in more ancient vernacular, Mars could be said to "rule" the canine species. (Perhaps with the help of Mercury or Jupiter thrown in, depending on the breed and size of the dog.)

Every two and half years, like clockwork, Mars crosses over my *"South Lunar Node,"* a curious point in the horoscope representing loss (and much else besides). Astrologers have nicknamed this point "The Dragon's Tail" in the chart.

For a large part of my life, each time Mars has reached this fascinating point in my very own chart, a similar event has occurred. Every time the planetary configuration would line up, I would be out walking or bicycling, only to encounter a dead dog in the street.

Experience does in fact breed wisdom, and I finally got wise to the pattern. Here came Mars again, hurling through the sky about to cross over the place inhabited by my birth day's *South Node*.

"I've had enough of dead dogs!" thought I, resolving to stay home this time around. I found a good book, and seated myself amicably on the top stair of a weathered staircase overlooking a secluded backyard. It should be mentioned that for many years I had sat on these same familiar steps looking out onto my backyard without

mishap. I nibbled on some grapes and began what promised to be a pleasant afternoon, well quarantined from my peculiar problem.

Not ten minutes had transpired when two little pigtailed heads popped over the neighbors fence, franticly waving to me and calling out, *"Help us! A dog is dying in our backyard!"*

These two little girls were entirely unknown to me, and apparently the expiring canine was unknown to them. Despite living here for three years, I had never seen either these girls nor this dog before.

The rest of my afternoon was occupied with a slowly fading geriatric poodle and the rather brusque local dog rescue officer. The poor old pooch left the earthly veil shortly after he was carried away.

So much for my attempt to avert this curiously repeating cycle of Mars in my affairs! *"Hmmm..."* I thought, *"so if I cannot avoid the aspect, how can I re-channel the energy for a positive outcome?"* Two and half years later, Mars was again due to traverse over the place of my South Lunar Node.

Highly skilled astrologers are aware of useful techniques for re-channeling negative energy into a positive use of that particular vibration! Attempts to work with and heal problem vibrations in the chart are known by astrologers as "astrological remedials." My co-author

Andrea has written a remarkable book on this very subject!

OK, so how could I change a dog-death vibration? I diagnosed the negative planetary energy field at work and resolved the problem by inventing a positive activity to replace the same energies. I made sure that the positive activity selected would act to reverse, modify, or neutralize the negative trend, (whichever seemed to be the most fitting and reasonable choice).

After a little bit of study and a lot of thinking, I determined that collecting garbage on my block was a fitting "energy trade" for encountering dead dogs. Just how the act of collecting garbage was to remedy my dead-dog problem involves a type of thinking lost to this century. I'll attempt to explain it to you.

We see here that Mars is crossing the South Lunar Node. Mars traditionally "governs" dogs, yes, but Mars also governs muscular activity. The South Node is that great exit point of the universe, where forms leave manifestation. For our purposes here, it can metaphorically represent garbage. The logic here is that if I were to extend my physical energy (Mars) in tossing things out, (South Node), the astrological energy exchange (from negative to positive) would be complete. Voila!

Also, The South Node traditionally demands a selfless sacrifice. Garbage collecting is one of those thankless jobs that other people seem to benefit from, but often fail to recognize. Thus, cleaning up junk while Mars passed my South Node became the ideal trade for my persistent dead dog problem. What was the result of my energy re-channeling experiment?

Ever since I began collecting garbage on my block, no more dead dogs have landed in my path when Mars visits my South Lunar Node.

OPERA BABY

I don't know if you believe in past lives. But even if you don't, the story that follows is an interesting one!

When reading charts, I rarely allow a baby in the office. For one, this often means that the parent will have a hard time focusing, and secondly, babies can at times tend to shriek. The piercing noise of an unhappy baby can easily dislodge the delicate sensitivities that are so necessary in order to do a good chart reading.

I will never forget the day when a very special baby named Naftali arrived in my office. Naftali was an obese baby, round as an onion. He was strapped lovingly to an extremely lean mother. *"He won't be any trouble at all."* She promised. *"He's a quiet sort of infant. Doesn't fuss at all. He's preverbal."* I wasn't so sure about his mother's promise. Ninety minutes is an eternity for an infant!

Naftali was almost a year old, perhaps 10 months. Indeed, he was preverbal. Let me emphasize "preverbal." He couldn't speak yet, and made few sounds. He didn't even gurgle! Naftali, his mother, and I sat at the table so that I could read the birth chart of the little lad.

During the chart reading of a baby or a child, the parent is provided with an useful blueprint of their wee one's strengths, weakness, vocational aptitudes and health tendencies. I always tell Mom and Dad:

"Your child's character is much like a garden. In this garden are the pre-existing seeds of both weeds and roses. Its your job to clip the weeds and encourage the roses."

So there he sat, perched on Mom's lap, strangely attentive but quite silent. However, unlike most infants Naftali seemed to have some definite sense that we were discussing his life and character. His focused on my words, and sat at perfect attention.

Naftali's reading went along as usual for most of the ninety minute session. Not a peep out of the little lad. Frankly, his persistent silence was a little bit eerie. Finally I said to his mother, *"I don't know if you believe in past lives, but Naftali's chart shows three testimonies of having possibly been an opera singer in a recent past life."*

No sooner had these words escaped my lips than the strangely silent baby opened his mouth and began to sing! He emitted a long, carefully sustained note.

His note was nothing resembling an infant's gurgling or experimental yells. This was a trained, carefully sustained single note, held at perfect pitch. Being a musician, I sure know the difference! As he sang, he stared intently into my eyes.

Needless to say, Naftali's mother and I were stunned. It was completely clear that Naftali knew exactly what I had said, and was agreeing with this assessment in the only way he could. Now how can a baby this young know what I had inferred about his past life, much less understand the words *Opera Singer*? We could point to recent studies proving that infants know a whole lot more words then we imagine they do, long before they actually speak!

There was no doubt in either my mind, or his mother's that Naftali knew *exactly* what I'd said, and that he had given us his best attempt at Pavarotti!

For the remainder of his long reading, Naftali made not one tiny sound.

SCREAMING REDHEAD

It was a typically foggy San Francisco afternoon, with the scent of Eucalyptus hanging in the air. I received a call from Talia, a self employed artist and concerned mother of a three month old redheaded infant. Talia's baby just would not sleep, and instead kept on screaming.

Sure, babies can tend to scream. But not like this. Poor Talia and her husband had reached a point of extreme sleep deprivation. Fortunately, Talia knew the exact minute of little Tymmons' birth, a fact of incalculable value to those who can read the constitutional energies of the cosmos. Once I had taken the time to draw up a map of where the planets were at the moment of baby Tymmons' birth, and it was quite easy to see the problem.

Not only did the chart show that Tymmons had a constitution that was composed of all active or *masculine* signs, but it also indicated that he had been born with an excess of planets in the hot fiery signs. To compound matters, he took his first breath as the red planet Mars was exactly rising at birth, shining on his body from the east and imbuing him with even more heat. This eastern horizon is the "place of honor" in the horoscope, and Mars was sitting right there!

The old astrologers divided the zodiac signs into four elemental groups: *Fiery, Watery, Earthly* and *Airy*. The athletic Fire sign trio of *Aries, Leo* and *Sagittarius* are energetically wide awake, whereas the Water sign trio produces a sleepy vibration especially in the case of Pisces and Cancer. Any person can verify this seasonal variation for themselves by comparing the birth dates of their more dreamy and gentle friends with their more hyperactive and/or extroverted companions.

As I considered the chart, it had become obvious that little redheaded Tymmons possessed a hyper-masculine, fiery birth chart with a hot Mars "ruling" the horoscope. Stranger still, Mars is the planet of redheads, but that is another story!

No wonder he was screaming! Little Tymmons was overheated with hot, dry energy. Immediately, I suspected dehydration and hyperactivity.

"Does Tymmons suffer from dehydration?" I quizzed Talia.

"Oh Yes!" she replied, *"he was so dehydrated at birth that they kept him an extra three days in the hospital to hydrate him!"*

Pacing the floor, I recalled the old energetic remedials of Renaissance physicians. An idea burst into my mind. How clear, how simple, how sweet.

"Water! Water is the perfect antidote for Fire! A fiery redhead born under Mars is dehydrated."

I thought that if real water were applied, it would soothe and balance the excessive heat that Tymmons was producing.

"Talia, why not try bathing Tymmons before he goes to bed? See what happens."

The story goes that Talia called two weeks later relating that her little redhead absolutely loves his bedtime bath. The before bed time baths had stopped the screaming and Tymmons now sleeps normally. And best of all, so does his mother Talia!

THE COMPUTER WIFE

In the early 1980s, at a time when computer addiction was still considered a recognized illness, I received a pleading call.

"I want to have a baby, but my husband won't get off the computer. Its been seven years, and heaven knows, we have tried. Can you help me?"

It was just my luck to have in my library a unique book entitled *Astrological Birth Control Fertility*. This priceless book described the methods developed by doctor Eugen Jonas in Nitra, Czechoslovakia. His renowned clinic once used Astrology to cure infertility, claiming 80% success with "infertile" women, and 80% success at gender prediction. Using astrological methods in combination with Jonas' lunar based fertility models, I calculated the charts of Lillian and her computer enslaved husband.

Lillian climbed into her plush, silver Mercedes and sped to my tiny office in Berkeley, California. She was an unusually attractive woman in her thirties, tastefully attired. One wondered why her husband preferred the computer! Her eyes shone with a longing for the one thing that alluded her: a baby. Carefully, I studied the positions of the Moon, Mars and Venus. Neither of the couple's charts showed any evidence of infertility. This was not the problem.

"Tonight," I insisted,*"tonight, at 7:15 p.m., you are at optimum fertility. The chances of conceiving a boy are very high."*

"Oh, we do want a boy!" Lillian responded. *"But I am not ovulating."*

"Well, according to your internal celestial time clock, tonight's the night. You see Lillian, the Czech physicians discovered that many women ovulate twice a month. Once at their "expected' ovulation time, and again when the Moon returns to the phase she held during the minute that woman was being born."

"That's impossible!" replied Lillian.

"I think you should try it anyway," I continued, *"The Jonas Clinic reported that over 75% of their successful pregnancies*

occurred during the moment of highest astrological fertility and __not__ at the standard monthly ovulation time! Tonight's your night, 7:15 p.m. sharp."

"OK, I'll see what I can do," Lillian agreed, heading out the door with renewed hope.

A short while later I received Lillian's report. She enticed her husband off his computer that very night, at precisely 7:15 p.m. as advised. Their romantic rendezvous resulted in a successful conception! Now we must remember that this success had occurred after a seven year infertility streak!

Nine months later, Lillian gave birth to an exceptionally handsome son with a big head of chestnut curls.

Although this story has many repeats, I am still astonished at the great help the planets can lend to "infertile" couples. Maybe the Moon knows more about women than thermometers?

BEGINNER'S LUCK

Astrologers can't always read a birth chart. Just like any other kind of detective, sometimes we are stumped. Perhaps we cannot read a chart if a client really does not want us to...but that's just a theory. I am now thinking back to a time I was stumped indeed. On this particular day, I spent the morning pacing around my office in bedroom slippers, pondering the chart in my hand, yet I remained completely flummoxed. A certain woman was due that week for an appointment and I could not get any information from her chart. The planets were there, but for some strange reason, they didn't speak to me.

My apprentice Janet was visiting. She was a cheerful, round Italian woman of exquisite intelligence and superlative wit. *"What do you think?"* I asked. *"Want to try your hand at this? Can you see anything here?"* I handed her the chart in the same way a doctor might ask to borrow the eyes of a bright intern in order to get help reading a cat scan that puzzled him.

She studied the chart for not more then a few minutes before brightly announcing, *"I think she will be very fat!"*

"That's all?" I asked. *"Anything else?"*

"It's all I can see," she replied. *"I keep looking, but that is all I can see! Its overwhelming."*

Janet abruptly handed the chart back to me and went on about her day's business.

What an odd pronouncement from the lips of a "greenhorn" whom had never yet read a chart. Although her evaluation was of little help to me, it was indeed a spontaneous outburst of exceptional interest.

The day of the appointment came around, and I heard the heavy footfalls coming up the steps, and then, a knock upon the door.

Before me stood the largest person to ever grace my offices, before or since. From her appearance, I would guess that she topped the scales at over five hundred pounds. My largest client's chair was just too small. I hauled my spacious oakwood rocking chair into the office and began the reading, still fishing for something useful to say.

Twenty years have come and gone since the day of that reading, but I still muse at the accuracy of Janet's pronouncement. Call it beginner's luck if you like. Call it intuition. Or coincidence. As for me, I prefer to celebrate a sincere student's well performed *cosmobiological* analysis.

SKY ROCKS

Every few years we see the introduction of new careers. As a vocational astrologer, it is sometimes difficult to keep up with all that's new in the job market. This story is an amusing example of this phenomenon of changing trends in the work force.

Over twenty years ago, my neighbor Bill employed my services in order to read the chart of his fourteen year old daughter Rebecca.

During a natal reading, we look at strengths, weaknesses, talents, and all manner of useful information that a parent might wish to know about their child. And no, babies are not exactly "blank slates" at birth. Astrology tells us that we each possess our own unique proclivities right from the moment of birth.

I happen to be one of those astrologers who sees the potential vocational applications of planetary patterns.

I'm not so concerned with the psychological interpretations of birth charts, but rather I tend to ask the question, *"What is this person good for?"* This comes naturally to me in a process that occurs the minute I engage a horoscope. It is as if I am wired to see how a person's character is best applied. Above all, it is my belief that Astrology should be useful!

Some folks are born to be cooks and others are made to be coroners. Apple trees grow apples and pear trees grow pears. Why shouldn't each birth moment produce its own unique vocational potentials?

So I looked at young Rebecca's chart, and when I did, her unique planetary birth pattern sang to me about the work she was born to do. However, this future vocation was a bit confounding to describe, because it made no sense to me.

"She will be studying the exacting details of physical objects, and earthy objects, but at a great, great distance." What on earth could this be? Just what were these "earthy objects?" I couldn't figure it. I struggled, trying to explain what I was seeing and feeling to Bill. The birth chart showed the drift but I could not match what I saw in the chart to any profession in my mental bank of possible careers.

"Its just as if she is doing this very tedious intricate work on earthy objects, but at the same time looking into vast distances, far, far away."

I had no internal reference to know precisely what Rebecca's future profession was to turn out to be. Maybe it hardly even existed at the time! Perhaps she would be working with some new type of geometry or geology performed on objects at a distance? I said as much to Bill, wishing I could be more precise.

Twenty some years flew by. Bill has since informed me that Rebecca obtained her college diploma in Planetary Geology, and is now a successful *Planetary Geologist* with a specialty in working at studying the planet Mars. She has spent years now in the tedious and exacting examination of the rocks and geological details of distant objects in the cosmos.

As a tiny seed contains the future tree it may one day become; the map of the planets at birth displays the potentials of a given life, and sometimes, as in Rebecca's case, this destiny is quite precise!

RUBY RED SLIPPERS

One by one I read the horoscopes of Eva's nordic sons (the family hailed from Stockholm). This sacred service was provided by phone when her sons were tiny tots. I never saw the boys in person. Eva was especially wise because she sought to understand her offspring's true character right at the starting gates of life.

Her last two or three sons (I cannot be sure of the number as this was some years ago) presented normative birth charts, describing the interests and athleticism typical to small boys. This news was all too harmonious with Dad, who was a "man's man" and an enthusiastic athlete. True to form, Eva's boys grew into soccer and baseball playing lads who fit well their father's expectations. Then along came Bjorn. He was probably three at the time that Eva contacted me.

As usual, I opened my *Ephemeris* and calculated a chart for the birth time and date of this latest arrival on the family scene. Right away, something was different about Bjorn's birth chart. It showed a character most feminine in nature. Our "ladies" of the celestial pantheon, the gentle Moon and sweet Venus, dominated the moment of his birth, plus there were other consistent testimonies of an overwhelmingly girlish disposition. Astrologers are used to this. We find human anomaly to be completely natural, and certainly not the parent's "fault."

We are born with innate qualities. Our uniqueness is reflected and explained by the planetary positions at birth. Genetic heritage is certainly a major part of our physical personality, but the planetary birth chart also describes the native qualities of the incoming soul (inherent qualities that exist within the child despite anything that could have been taught to the child by his or her parents).

Because I was uncertain as to how Eva might take this news, I broached the subject gently but with complete honesty.

"Bjorn will not be like his brothers. There are several testimonies that he is extremely feminine in both character and tastes."

His mother's response surprised me!

Rather then being disappointed by my news, Eva was seriously relieved!

"Well this explains it," she said *"Bjorn tantrums when we we will not buy him the fancy red velveteen girl's shoes with the sequins on them!"*

At age three, little Bjorn was already displaying unquestionably girlish tastes, at least in his footwear! He was born this way, just as promised in his planetary birth pattern.

Eva related that Bjorn's manly father was open to accepting his son's individuality. How fruitless it would be to force football on a soul whom was perhaps more destined for Broadway musicals!

An understanding of a child's inborn character as is promised in his/her natal chart can replace the usual confusion, blame or conflict that might occur for the parents in a case such as this. And this is just one example of how Astrology can help both children and their parents. In this case, young Bjorn could now go forth into a far more harmonious life than might have been expected otherwise.

MISS COMMUNICATIONS

In the 1990s I rented an office in the upstairs of an old Victorian house, above a popular bookstore in the Northwest. The walls were hung with portraits of Saints and Gurus. It always felt so peaceful working in the company of Saint Theresa, Paramansa Yogananda, and their fellows.

Today, I was studying a chart peculiar for its emphasis on Mercury, the planet of communication. Not only was this planet prominent, but it was heavily "afflicted" as we say in the old vernacular. Certainly, the woman I was about to meet must have experienced some sort of substantial issues with communication. Was it speech? Hearing? Writing? Or was it an inability to understand what was said to her, or vice versa, to be understood? Mercury rules speech, writing, and is strongly associated with the sense of hearing. I would have to wait and see just how her obvious Mercurial affliction might manifest!

There was a knock on my door, and in bolted a twenty-something Argentinean woman with long black hair, wearing a San Francisco Giants baseball cap and matching blue sweatshirt.

I welcomed her into the office and after our brief introductions, I began to read her chart. However, things did not go quite as usual. Every time I broached the question of "a problem with communicating," she would vehemently deny this possibility. I tried different approaches. *"Your chart shows an afflicted Mercury. Have you ever had trouble communicating?"*

"Not me," she would answer, as if puzzled by my words. Then, I would try a new angle.

"Perhaps you stuttered as small child? Or had a learning disability?"

"No," she said, *"I've never had any communication problems."*

"Were you slow to read? Are you dyslexic?"

"Nope, I've never had an issue with communicating!" I was persistent. This couldn't be possible!

"Have you ever had trouble understanding people, or being understood?"

"I don't think so!" she replied.

My line of questioning went on to no avail. Frankly, this was just plain weird. Charts are almost never wrong when one sees "three testimonies." And here before me were more than three! Did she give me an incorrect birth time? No, the birth time checked out. My predicament deepened because everything in her chart led back to this one theme - trouble with communication! A Mercury this severely afflicted could only mean that this woman suffered some form of serious communication malady. But what? She continued to deny that any such problem existed.

The reading ended. As I was seeing her out the door, she suddenly turned around and casually remarked over her shoulder,

"Oh, I forgot to tell you! I was stone deaf until I was eighteen years old, and then, was completely cured by an ear surgery. Bye!"

THE YOM KIPPUR TRAGEDY

In my thirties, I maintained a small office in Berkeley, California, on an old street near the college where cherry blossoms bloomed in winter. From my window, I watched the diverse gaggle of people, bikes and leash-less dogs passing far below. On one particular day, the phone interrupted my reverie. It was Saul Rueben, a brilliant comrade in Astro-Seismic Research.

He had an interesting request.

"My mom needs a rather routine knee surgery. Nothing dangerous really, but I thought I'd have you check it out anyway. The date is already set for Yom Kippur."

This announcement immediately raised my eyebrows. Every self respecting Jew knows that Yom Kippur is the holiest day of the year. Could this be an inauspicious warning?

I carefully constructed the chart of Saul's mom, a woman in her late seventies. The amount of "bad planetary aspects" occurring in this woman's chart on the precise date of her planned knee surgery were alarming.

Astrologers have long known that tension begins when a traveling planet (or as we say, a "transiting" planet) aligns in a ninety degree angle from a planet in the birth chart.

This 90 degree angle between two planets is called a "square." In the old books, the square aspect was always labeled as a "negative" influence. The Yom Kippur surgery date showed that almost every single planet was positioned in this "unlucky" ninety degree angle from its own position in the chart of the moment at which Saul's mother was born!

More specifically, the knee surgery date was planned ninety days forward from Saul's mom's birth date, or "square" to her birth Sun. She was also going to have traveling Mars square to her Mars, Venus square Venus, etc.

As if this wasn't enough, Saul's mom had a lot of tense configurations that were to be crossing through the sign of Capricorn on the day of surgery. The zodiacal sign of Capricorn is the sign that is said to "rule" the knees.

"Dear me!" I thought, *"This planned surgery date is dangerous, and must be averted!"*

I encouraged Saul to reschedule the surgery, but he responded that he had no power to do so. The decision was his father's, who was handling everything in regards to the surgery for his mother. Of course, Saul said that he would mention the problem to his father. Sadly, Saul's Dad never breathed one word of my dire concern to Saul's mother. Neither did he change the unfortunate date of her surgery.

Saul's Dad was probably a member of that fraternity of folks that think Astrology is "silly," or perhaps "occult" or worse, evil. It is unfortunate at times like this that Cosmos-biology (Astrology) is erroneously believed to be an occult activity. Checking into the surgery date of Saul's mother in this case is no more occult than the general act of predicting the weather.

Cosmos-biology is certainly not silly, and of course it is no more evil than electrical engineering. Be that as it may, I thought it most unfortunate that Saul's money was wasted upon my services, as my insights were ignored. The Yom Kippur surgery was not stopped and you might well be wondering what happened.

Saul's mother suffered a stroke and a heart attack during the operation. She died shortly thereafter, as a result of the surprising complications incurred during her routine and "harmless" knee surgery. The physicians of the Renaissance would never have made this egregious mistake in surgical timing!

Let's hope for that fine day when once again, the cosmobiological influences, as shown in the horoscope, are consulted before entering into the surgeon's lair.

THE DAY IS NOT YET OVER

The arrival of good fortune can definitely be seen in a person's birth chart, though this good luck itself is seldom unearned. If one believes in karma, (the unavoidable law of cause and effect), then luck as we know it is not really an accident. Rather, it could be said that fortune arrives when the seeds of our good karma sprout. These are seeds that we have buried long ago in our gardens, with our very own hands! And just like seeds, our luck sprouts when the weather of a particular time period is perfect for the growth of that particular seed. Its all about timing. And of course timing is all about the planets!

Divine Grace, on the other hand, could be described as the occurrence of divine intervention. This kind of luck or reprieve *also* exists, though *divine intervention* is probably a subject better suited for another discussion! But for now, let us just say that Grace itself operates *outside of, and above* the planetary weather, though is in itself so often presaged by the arrival of that great messenger of Grace, Jupiter.

It is true that the planets can foretell certain times of exceptionally lucky weather. Naturally, the reverse is also true in regards to misfortune. At times, the planets can show a time period that is decisively unlucky for a certain person or nation.

This however is a happy tale so let's get back to favorable times of luck and grace. Years ago, as the date had just rolled over to 2000, I was invited to speak at a conference in Las Vegas being held by the *American Federation of Astrologers*. I'd never been to Las Vegas before, and was not prepared for the wall of heat that hit me like a sack of beans when I stepped off the plane.

"The Astrologer's Convention please," I instructed the gum chewing taxi driver. It was amazing how many nationally known astrologers of all shapes and sizes were converging on the scene of the packed conference. It was all so exciting! I was especially excited, because I had peeked into my *Ephemeris* before departing. The *Ephemeris* is the astrologer's handy pocket guide of current planetary placements, and is a primary tool for any working astrologer. When I had flipped through the pages of *The Ephemeris*, I had noticed that the planets were about to pile up in a manner that promised to be one of the most fortunate days of my entire life!

When reaching my room, I called my publisher. *"Make sure you push my new book tomorrow,"* I encouraged her. *"It is my super lucky day for books. I am sure we will get an offer!"*

You are probably wondering how I could tell that this next day was to be so fortunate. Jupiter is the planet that tends to bring about lucky weather. As astrologers, we tend to call Jupiter the "Great Benefic," as Jupiter tends to bring feelings of being glorious and blessed. Let's just say that when I looked into *The Ephemeris*, I noticed that Jupiter would be supremely prominent on the next day, poised to deliver his blessing.

But again, we can ask the question; how does this planetary ebullience even work?

It could be said that Jupiter does not necessarily "cause" good fortune. Rather, this process could be thought of in the way that Jupiter heralds the positive planetary weather that assists the seeds of hope and joy to sprout.

My garden of seeds had been planted, watered, and tended to at some point in the past. Jupiter's arrival signaled to me that my fruits were soon to be fully ripe and it was time to reap my reward. Tomorrow was the day! This could be likened to a field of pumpkin seeds, lying under the soil awaiting for the Sun to brightly shine. When this perfect time arrives the seedlings will sprout up from the ground, ready to produce pumpkins.

And why shouldn't there be planetary weather operating in the hidden spheres? Because I knew that Jupiter was coming, I was expectant. My fortune would be in publishing! Of this I was certain. Although Jupiter is generous to all concerns, it seemed apt that my fortune would be in books. After all, that was where I had planted my seeds. Besides, Jupiter traditionally "rules" publishing!

My plan was to attend this astrologer's conference just for fun. The morning dawned and began with its usual round of speakers. By 3 p.m., I was a bit disappointed by the fact that no luck had shown itself in what appeared to be a dismally normal day. I purchased a pearl from one of the vendors specializing in astrological remedials. Maybe that would help.

As I excitedly waited for something to happen, I had heard not one word from my publisher. In the hallway I encountered a tall and elegant gentleman named Bob Cooper, who so happened was the longtime President of the *American Federation of Astrologers*, now in his eighties. He graciously asked if I would be attending tonight's gala dinner event. The banquet dinner was a fancy affair, full on with a performance by an astrological theatre troupe. Plates were $50 a head, which was one hefty price for a young astrologer like myself.

"I'm sorry," I replied, *"I really can't afford the ticket."*

"But you certainly must come!" Bob urged. *"When you arrive, look for me and be my guest. You really must be there!"*

Dinnertime arrived and I found my way to the enormous auditorium. On my way down, I had shared the crammed elevator with what appeared to be a group of prostitutes on the way to their own convention. It was 6 p.m. and the day nearly over. Still no luck. Not one piece of good news had arrived from the publishing world on this supposedly special day. Frankly, I was dismayed.

Would Jupiter really let me down this badly? Dinner came for the astrologers, and then began what seemed like hours of intensely boring (to me) astro-drama and other entertainment. By this time it was 9 p.m.

Inside I was thinking that surely the stars had been wrong. No fortune would be mine on what had become a disappointing day. One by one, the astrologers filtered and drifted out of the room, back to their hotel rooms high above the wild gambling tables. I sat there perplexed, as my faith in Jupiter was sorely challenged. It was at this juncture that I recalled the words of my beloved father, who had been the person to first teach me Astrology. At times such as this, he would say to me,

"The day is not yet over."

In honor of these provocative words, we will now briefly diverge into a colorful story *within* our story!

While serving as a private during World War Two at the Presidio in San Francisco, my father's interest in Astrology became known amongst the curious young officers. One day a young Sergeant approached him for a reading. Dad gave the officer a precise date and explained that this was the day he would receive the promotion he so desperately had wanted. And not just a promotion, but something else he wanted very much besides! The promised lucky day arrived. At about three in the afternoon, the Sergeant burst in upon my father and rather mockingly said something like,

"Well Hill, looks like this Astrology of yours doesn't work!"

When relaying this story to me, my father had explained that in this moment, he looked up unfazed from his desk and cooly replied,

"The day is not yet over."

At 5:30 p.m., the Sergeant reappeared, looking a bit sheepish. Not only had he received the promotion he had so hoped for, but something else he wanted very much besides!

Down the years my father's memorable words have heartened me, and today I recalled them back to mind once more.

"The day is not yet over indeed," I repeated, *"let us wait and see."*

The AFA dinner hall was now emptying fast when at 9:30 p.m., the emcee announced that we were about to have an *AFA, Inc.* awards presentation. At this late point in the evening, I sat alone at an empty table sipping tepid water. Over half the guests had now retired to their rooms. The dull quiet that filled the spacious hall was broken by these words:

"And now we are pleased to present our winner of the Paul R. Grell Award for the Best Book among all of the AFA Publications for 1999..."

(drum rolls)

*"We would like to present this award to Judith Hill for her latest book entitled **Vocational Astrology**"*

Needless to say, I nearly choked on my water.

My father's words had rang true once again! That evening ended with me climbing up onto the stage in order to accept a plaque commemorating the award, which proudly hangs to this day on my office wall.

That day turned out to be one of the luckiest days of my life after all.

Jupiter delivered his good fortune in publishing as promised in my birth chart, exactly right on time!

STELLAR RESCUE

Mose McKinley was a good looking and magnetic man. Interested women buzzed around him like bees around a fruit cake. He was also an amateur astrologer whom I came to casually know within the circles of our local state Astrologer's Association.

He called me one morning just as I was scrambling down breakfast.

"Listen," he began in a voice full of concern, *"I've an urgent decision to make involving my health. The doctors want to perform an exploratory surgery on my intestines to see what's wrong. We can do this before or after my planned month long vacation cruise. Do you think it can wait a*

month? Or should I arrange for surgery right away? You see, I am so looking forward to my long awaited Hawaiian holiday!"

Hurriedly, I constructed his birth chart based on his time, date, place and year of birth. What I saw alarmed me!

Now I've seen a whole lot of horoscopes, and know how to weigh the intensity and seriousness of a set of "transits," i.e. planetary beams shining upon a client's birth chart.

Analyzing the manner in which the currently moving planets mix with the birth chart pattern is not that much different then analyzing radio signals or sonic tones. I busied myself in observing the planetary weather in Mose's health chart.

So what did I see that so concerned me, above and beyond your usual set of weekly transits?

Mose's chart showed probable death within two days! This was strikingly clear without a doubt. However, here was a first rate interpretive dilemma. Was the danger from having surgery? Or from *not* having the surgery?

Occasionally, astrologers are confronted with conundrums of this sort!

Obviously, this was a critical judgement call. I adjudicated that since he was planning to go forward with his Hawaiian vacation, this danger was then in *not* urgently pursuing the exploratory surgery. But still, one cannot be too certain, ever.

"Mose," I said, *"Here's the deal. Your chart has several indications from Pluto, Saturn, and Mars. This planetary configuration suggests that events might reach a crisis point within two days."* I went on to explain my interpretive dilemma and inquired as to what his physician advised. Apparently, Mose's physicians were entirely unaware of the imminent danger looming, so clearly shouting warning signals from Mose's birth chart. Instead, the doctors had blithely placed in Mose's own hands the decision between a pre-holiday or post-holiday surgery.

"It is my opinion that you should not play around with such loud planetary warnings. If your doctor agrees, have the surgery immediately."

Being a "believer," Mose wasted no time arranging an immediate surgery. On the table, the surgeons opened him up and to their surprise discovered a badly perforated intestine.

When he awakened, his physicians informed him that if he hadn't gone into immediate surgery, he most probably would have died within forty eight hours.

Saved by the testament of the stars, missing his boat to Hawaii was now the last thing on Mose's mind.

THE HORSE'S KNEES

Violette Dunn is one of the dandiest horsewomen in these parts. She teaches horses to dance, and possesses a special affection for Thoroughbreds. Violette always arrived exquisitely attired in tight fitting designer clothes, bearing gourmet treats for the astrologer. I nicknamed her "The Duchess" and have never met a woman with more poise, nor a stronger will. Violette was currently preoccupied with the purchase of the gelding "Roquefort." She wondered if a horse's chart could be anything like a human's chart, and if so, would I please consider charting him before she invested a large sum on his purchase.

"I really don't know," I said fascinated. *"We can try!"*

After all, why wouldn't a horse's horoscope work just like the chart of a person? Horses share with us four limbs, a head, nose, eyes, and ears. Both species share similar emotions and individual variances of temperament. As far as I am concerned, horses are people too.

"Excellent," she said, collecting her exquisite black purse, *"call me when you are ready."*

I decided to approach the interpretation of Roquefort the Horse's birth chart in the same manner as I would for a person's nativity. Still, he wasn't a human person, so just how might I accomplish this? The chart was calculated for his birth time, date, year and place, same as for any human. What I saw intrigued me. Roquefort was born with a badly afflicted cluster of planets in Capricorn.

"The knees," I thought, *"Capricorn rules the knees. This horse must have a significant delicacy of the knees."* Looking further, I saw that he was likely also to be malnourished and emaciated. Additionally, Roqueforte should never be boarded in the same paddock with Violette's gelding, Tom, whose chart was also drawn.

The two horses both had their Mars positions tied closely in the same boisterous sign of Aries. If they roomed too closely they would go delinquent, just like two teenage boys in a league of high spirits.

The day of the appointment arrived, and I shared my insights with "Vee," knowing full well that we both were testing Astrology.

"Roquefort has delicate knees," I warned, *"plus he is malnourished. Secondly, he should never be boarded near Tom lest they bust out of their stalls or worse."*

Violette confided that Roquefort was indeed underweight and badly malnourished. He would require a devoted tenderness to put him right. Plus, his knees were so sensitive that they needed to warm them before riding. But despite my opinion, she was determined about boarding him in the same paddock as Tom.

A short time later, Roqueforte and Tom ran off together, getting themselves into some barbed wire. Fortunately, neither was badly injured. As for me, I was satisfied to learn that horses' birth charts work just fine!

BORN THAT WAY

To this day, there exist a great number of questions in regards to personal temperament and life choices. For instance, people often discuss the *nature vs nurture* argument in regards to homosexuality. The question is often asked of whether or not a person *chooses* to be gay.

The argument goes back and forth with nobody thinking of asking the opinion of the birth chart. After all, astrologers are specialists in the subject of *nature vs nurture*! The analysis and description of a person's inborn character is a large part of our work! These innate qualities fit within the *nature* part of the equation, but in this case they are not always due to genetics. Well reflected in the birth chart, let us call them *"the soul's contribution."*

It is curious that both sides of the nature-nurture debate neglect the prenatal existence of a human spirit! In this discussion "nature" typically refers to the genetic directives of the physical body, whereas "nurture" refers to the formative impact of parental and cultural influences. The birth chart describes both these things and something else besides! Where are described the inherent qualities of the human spirit? In the natal chart!

The balance between nature and nurture varies a great deal between individuals. Children born with forceful character may well resist any form of character guidance. Other children are so easily moulded by the opinions and behaviors of those around them.

Astrologers rarely see a chart that does not indicate both the strength of natural character, as well as its dominant traits. The chart even goes so far as to reveal the strains and stresses between inborn character versus the parental and early home influences!

Traditionally, a planet that is rising on the eastern horizon at the moment of birth describes the dominant qualities of the incarnating soul. For those that subscribe to reincarnation theory, these powerful planets also suggest the prominent activities of recent lives. Those whom do not accept soul transmigration could think of the *rising planet* as somehow infusing the child's personality and destiny with the qualities of that planet.

The case file that follows is the fascinating study of *"nature vs. nurture."* Lynne was born at a moment during which the distinctly masculine planet of Mars was making his powerful eastern passage. And thus, the character of Mars has been very prominent within Lynne from the time that she was a tiny infant girl.

Lynne was born in the famous rodeo town of Pendleton, Oregon. Her loving parents are educated and respected members of their small community. As mentioned, Lynne was also born under the influence of the planet Mars, because "he" was making his eastern passage by rising upon the horizon at the moment of her birth. And thus, Mars was shining his hot and fiery rays upon her tiny newborn body at the time of her spirit's incarnation.

Most succinctly, it could be said that Mars is a warrior! Traditionally, he "rules" the red blood cells, the muscles, as well as our levels of testosterone and adrenalin. On account of the hot energies of Mars, this planet is also connected with weapons, tools, dogs, athletes and fighting men. Mars is never "girly"!

What ever could it mean then, for an infant girl to be born exactly under the rising beams of Mars?

The story that follows here is a special treat. Let us step aside and allow Lynne to describe for us in her own words what life as a girl was like for her, a soul born into a female body precisely as the masculine planet of Mars dominated her birth moment.

As Lynne tells her own story:

"I was what, 3 years old or maybe 4? I can remember a day when my well-meaning mother tried to put me in a very scratchy yellow dress for some occasion, probably Easter. She had also permed my hair and bought me some patent leather shoes for my feet. I felt utterly horrible in an outfit such as this. I felt awful not just from being all dressed up in the Eastern Oregon heat, but more from being dressed up like some girl-doll. I was not that kind of girl and I never would be. Pleeease! Let me wear my shorts and tennis shoes! I wanted to wear my jeans and cowboy hat and six-shooter!

I wrestled, cried and struggled every time that my mother tried to get any kind of skirt on me. I would quickly remove them for a more normal outfit of coveralls and a cap and sneakers. Mismatched socks and cotton jacket. And of course the six-shooter (one must accessorize properly). Finally, my dad said to my sweet but frustrated mother, "*What does it matter? She has clothes on; who cares what they are?!*"

So went the remainder of my childhood fight about the "proper attire for a girl." As I became older and attended school, we had a dress code. And when I say this I literally mean a "dress" code. In grade school, I had to obey these byzantine laws until they were gradually retracted by the time I entered into my high school years. All the while my skinny legs froze while I tried to navigate the monkey bars and the see-saw, or while I was trying to participate in a decent game of kickball. This is nearly impossible in a dress, a skirt, or a jumper. I left for school each morning mortified that I had to wear this crap, while the boys dashed about in more sensible trousers and sweatshirts. The girls inevitably stood around, looking on from the side in mini-skirts and go-go boots (*remember those*?!).

At last, having grown into my young adult life, I was able to dress in a natural way. My preferred style of dress was pin-stripe suits, dress shirts, bow-ties and leather motorcycle jackets. I had long ago learned how to tie a necktie, fitting it neatly into my oxford shirt. I spent my time studying *Esquire* and *Gentleman's Quarterly* for style tips. Not that finding clothes for my slight 5-foot-3 build was easy; but I never did learn or fit into women's garments. Was I an 8 or a 10? Did I want this in pink or teal? God, no! I prefer to ask questions such as:

Don't you have these wing-tips in size 3?

*Can't you see these chinos are completely too wide in the hips
for me, not to mention lacking in real pockets?*

I still made the occasional stab at a feminine appearance.
The first woman I married dressed similarly to me; she
wore silk blouses and long linen skirts. I felt awkward on
many fronts, though delighted to have a kind partner at
last who exchanged vows with me (our marriage occurred
in the 1980s, a time when few gay women would partake
in a "heterosexual institution" such as this).

Around the time of my first marriage was when I wore a
skirt for the last time. I promised myself to never go down
that road again, no matter what the consequences might
be. People would ask *"Why are you so masculine?"* I also
heard this question, *"If you wish you were a man so much,
why don't you just get a sex change?"* I struggle to this very
day about how to answer the latter question. At this point,
I tend to say something like,

*"I'm still female, just a different kind of female. It's not about
rearranging body parts; it's about the clothes I put on. And
please, when you stick me in my coffin, make sure my tuxedo is
nicely pressed."*

ANKLE FANDANKLE

I will never forget the day that Gina's daughter contacted me regarding her mother's condition. She imparted to me that five doctors had failed to discover the cause of mother's mysterious ailment. Perhaps *Cosmos-biology* could be of some service in diagnosing the true problem.

Now isn't it remarkable how different you feel when I say *Cosmos-biology* instead of "Astrology?" The word "Astrology", seems to summon up archetypes of mumbling occultists in pointed hats. Others recall their 1960's memories of stoned out hippies bleating *"What's your sign?"* The many false associations attached to the word Astrology can cause some people to suffer from what my co-author Andrea terms *astrophobia*.

What an unfortunate state of cultural affairs!

Astrophobia in general prevents us westerners from enjoying the remarkable technology of Cosmos-biology. As mentioned, most of us are unaware that all through the Elizabethan era no doctor could be licensed without passing his exams in Cosmos-biology!

For these Renaissance doctors, the act of giving a diagnoses, timing events, and treatment selection were all topics to be considered through an examination of their patient's planetary birth chart. Cosmos-biology was an essential limb of any good medical practice!

Somehow Gina's daughter had escaped over the wall of cultural astrophobia and into my office.

"My mom has such painful feet that she can barely walk. She has been to multiple doctors but nobody can figure out what the problem is. She is being driven out of her mind and hardly wants to go on living. Astrology is my last resort!"

I explained that I was not a licensed physician and could legally neither diagnose the problem or prescribe medicine. However, what I could do was to give her a "lesson" in Renaissance medicine using her mom's chart as a hypothetical example. Any insights gleaned from the lesson could then be run by her mother's physician. She agreed.

I calculated Gina's planetary birth chart. After completing my research, I contacted Gina by phone. We chatted politely and settled into the lesson.

"A Renaissance physician would say that there are no planets in the sign of the feet, so the problem would not originate from the feet."

Gina responded with enhanced curiosity.

"That could make sense because five doctors now cannot yet find the cause of the intense foot pain. Maybe they were looking in the wrong place!"

I continued on with her lesson regarding this ancient medical model:

"You was born when Saturn, the planet of restriction, was in the last third of Aquarius. This is the sign "decan" that specifically governs the ankles. Looking at this chart picture, Nostradamus himself might assume that her ankles are to blame! There would appear to be some restriction in the ankles. Perhaps stenosis? The foot pain would be seen as not originating in the foot itself, being instead referred from the ankle."

Ankle *stenosis* means that the channel for the nerves in the ankle are too narrow. This structural tightness could cause an impingement of the nerves. This, in turn, might underly the intense pain in Gina's feet. At the point that Gina consulted me, I had never heard of ankle stenosis. I simply read the astrological chart Renaissance style, exactly as I saw it. We ambled on, studying the chart from many angles. Finally the lesson in ancient medical methodologies was over.

Gina's daughter called back a month or two later, sounding delighted.

"You were right!" she gleefully reported.

"Mom explained your idea to her podiatrist who did some tests. She does have ankle stenosis! He was able to shift some things and now the pain is gone. Gone! This is the first time in twenty years she has been pain free!"

It was to the considerable credit of this rare podiatrist that he didn't suffer from an astrophobia-induced stenosis of the ears.

THE RIGHT TIME

My student Paul was having an endlessly difficult time selling his gorgeous home in the damply beautiful NW Portland hills. Because it wasn't a slow period for real estate sales, it was puzzling how this impeccable house could have languished on the market now for over a year. Paul was a realtor himself, and he couldn't fathom what was causing this long delay. Everything was tried to enhance this property's sales appeal and attract buyers, but nevertheless, the house remained as if invisible.

As a last resort, Paul called me for help. Perhaps this was a good choice, because I was one of the few astrologers at the time who had studied "Electional Astrology", an ancient branch of knowledge dedicated to the art of timing important life ventures.

It just so happened that I had also had some experience in the highly specialized art of planning real estate sales according to the art and science of planetary timing.

The premises of selecting good startup times is simple:

The throw of the stone marks its course.

In my twenties, I had opened a small maverick business called "The Right Time." My logo was composed of a clock surrounded by planetary trajectories. This logo even ran in a popular magazine at the time! It never attracted more then two customers, a fact that puzzles me to this day.

Could it have been *astrophobia*? While I still to this day do not know the reason for this public disinterest in auspicious timing, I do know that many potential customers were missing out on the great blessing of right timing for their most important events. This could include the timing for marriages, surgeries, business openings, school exams, child conceptions, farming, and every other important event that might occur throughout the course of a given lifetime.

So here was an exasperated realtor, requesting my help in selling his home. Yay! I could finally put my strange knowledge to good use.

"First, let's take a look at the day you listed the home!"

As requested, Paul supplied the date that he had first listed the house. To no surprise of mine, it was an awful choice. No wonder the house had sat there for months as if it was invisible to buyers!

"What date did you purchase the home?" I asked.

This information would allow me to precisely identify this house in Paul's own horoscope.

He willingly complied.

I rolled up my shirt sleeves and went to work. I gathered up some pens, a ruler, a Golden Delicious apple, a few books, Paul's birth chart, the date of the house purchase, and the home listing charts. I sat down among the objects that now blanketed my desk.

Timing events correctly is a serious business often requiring hours of intense concentration. The calming sound of the Portland rain pounding the sidewalks helps me to focus. Thus, I began my careful search. After a few hours I found it. *"The Right Time!"*

The Sun, Moon, and all the planets were amicably arranged in just the right position in order to invite a sale. One might say that the planetary weather was *just right.*

Carefully, I'd set the Ascendant at zero degrees Aries. This would insure instant public response, as well as high visibility. Using the point of "Zero Aries" for a quick sales is a trade secret of mine. It is sort of like stirring the sunrise and the first minute of spring all together with a spoon, in order to create a successful re-listing minute for the home.

Good timing helps so much. After all, the course of an arrow's flight is marked at the moment it leaves the bow!

Such is the law of right timing.

"Paul, now here is what I want you to do. Take the house off the market completely. Then, at exactly 12:43 p.m. on this particular date, re-list the house. Use an atomic clock, and be precise. Make sure your realtor is on board."

Paul carried out my instructions to the letter. He removed his house from the market and re-listed it at the astrologically appointed minute of time. So, what happened?

Paul's home sold in hours, exactly for his asking price!

THE TOURIST

Ben Brownlow is a business man and a wee bit of a philanthropist. He regularly visited my tiny office situated high up in an old Victorian mansion. It was the year 1997, and time for another one of his yearly adventures.

"I've a ticket to Egypt," he cheerily explained. *"Can you check my itinerary to see if everything looks safe?"*

Now, I just love a good astrological detective job. Out came my pens and rulers. On came the fifties pop music that seems to help me focus. First, I drew up Ben's location charts for his planned arrival and departure points.

Where exactly were the planets in Cairo, Egypt, when Ben was busy being born in Elkhorn, Montana? This concept may sound strange to you. But, doesn't your car's radio pick up some radio stations better in some directions than others? *Astrological Locality* charts work in a manner similar to radio reception! Planetary vibrations are similar to radio waves! In one town we receive strong signals from Venus, while Mercury comes in loudest just over that next hill.

Highly skilled astrologers can compare regions and describe the dominant astral influences of each specific location. So I drew up Mr. Brownlow's chart for Luxor, Egypt and was not pleased with what I saw. The planetary "radio stations" he picked up in Egypt looked bad. Not just bad, but terrible.

I was surprised and disappointed. How could I bring myself to advise Ben against his life long dream of visiting the great and ancient land of the Pharaohs?

And, he already had made his reservation!

"OK then," I thought to myself *"Although most tourists adore Egypt, it's clearly not Ben's personal best vacation spot. Will the current planetary transits be positive enough to offset the testimony of his location chart?"* I opened my Astrologer's Handy Pocket Guide, (better known as an Ephemeris) and looked up the current planetary motions for November, 1997. Ben's current planetary transits agreed in unison with his inauspicious Egyptian location chart. Both charts warned of significant danger during the exact dates and place of his proposed holiday. Worse, the "bad" aspects came to the angles of the chart representing his point of arrival. I'd seen this before and know what charts looks like when folks narrowly escape being shipped home in a coffin!

To Ben's great fortune, he listened to my verdict: *"Egypt is extremely dangerous for you during November of this year."*

"I'll cancel my tickets," said Ben. I felt kind of guilty, hoping I did not needlessly ruin his fun. Ben later notified me that had he gone ahead with this trip, he would have been amongst the now renowned group of sixty two unsuspecting tourists who were shot by gunmen while viewing sights at Deir el-Bahri on November 17, 1997. Not everyone listens to planetary warnings. But after all, Ben Brownlow is a Pisces.

THE COSMIC MICROSCOPE

Astrologers can get too busy. Fortunately, we also know when to expect those days when everyone seems to call at once! It was one of those days. Today, I had already set one cataract surgery date, compared San Diego with Boston for relocation potential, and selected a few radio station employees. The phone rang again. *"Oy Vey,"* I thought, *"what now?"*

It was Candace, a popular young acupuncturist and practitioner of traditional Chinese medicine. She had an urgent problem. An inner prompt urged me to see her immediately, despite the fact that I was drowning in a sea of hurried requests. But hers seemed different.

She arrived at my Sellwood office where I had her chart prepared and waiting upon the consulting table. Rain was pattering on the windows. Candace explained how she was wasting away with some undiagnosable ailment. Several doctors found nothing (four or five as I recall). There was no evidence of bacteria or viral involvement.

All of the medical tests found nothing. And yet, she couldn't eat a thing and was surviving on slippery elm bark gruel. This had gone on for weeks, and simply could not go on much longer. A veritable coterie of doctors had proven useless in diagnosing the cause of this malady, and now she was truly fading away!

Retrieving her birth chart from the horoscope vaults, I applied myself to this baffling mystery.

Candace arrived at the appointed hour and we began.

As usual, I explained that I was not a licensed medical practitioner and could neither diagnose or prescribe. However, I could give her a lesson in Renaissance astrological techniques, using her chart as a hypothetical example.

"I understand completely," she said *"I'm a student of Astrology too."*

The planet Neptune appeared to be our culprit. Medically speaking, this astronomical "gas giant" rules over clouds, poisons, mold, fogs, gases and weird things we cannot see. He always turns up in mystery cases and misdiagnoses.

Just as I expected, Neptune had been dominating Candace's health chart over the last few weeks. Neptune was now moving exactly over Candace's birth "North Lunar Node," that special horoscopic doorway where cosmic energies enter into the body. The symbol of the North Node looks just like an upright horseshoe.

So here was the gas giant Neptune, parked on the exact spot where cosmic energies were entering into Candace's body; and also exactly on her Ascendant, that preeminent horoscopic point which represents her physical body. Neptune was currently in the "air" sign of Aquarius.

Medically speaking, Astrology can be quite literal. As in: air signs = oxygen. Neptune hints at secret poison. Now, all we need is the skill and training to read this celestial code!

"You may be absorbing hidden poison through the air," I suggested. *"Look into this immediately."*

Candace later admitted to me how she thought that this explanation was crazy, and that I was possibly nuts. She politely left my office, no doubt disappointed by the apparent futility of Medical Astrology.

However, weeks later some workmen came to fix something in her home. By happenstance, they discovered an ongoing carbon monoxide leak. They explained to her that only reason she wasn't dead, was because she slept with the window open! As noted, this was all precisely depicted in her birth chart: The mystery illness was caused by hidden poison in the air.

Modern doctors possess wonderful tools, such as microscopes and cat scans. But can these machines see into and describe the unseen energies of the cosmos?

DELUGE OF HAPPINESS

"Electional Astrology" is the remarkable art of choosing times for important events. *"To every thing there is a season, and time to every purpose under the heaven."* Ecclesiastes 3:1-8

Not so long ago, many of the most important political events were timed to the movement of the planets. Queen Elizabeth's coronation minute was expertly designed, much to the benefit of Britain! The Queen's advisor outdid himself. Viewing John Dee's famous coronation chart tells us that her reign was everything his carefully selected moment promised it to be.

Following in her footsteps, avid astrologer and American founding father George Washington, precisely timed the setting of the corner stones of the main buildings of our capital Washington D.C. He used in part, the rising times of Venus and Mercury.

Washington was not the last U.S. President to use planetary "elections" for important events. However, Ronald Reagan holds the distinction of the first president to get caught using Astrology! However, *Electional Astrology* is only one branch of the many useful, or "judicial" astrological sciences.

Predicting the weather by the planets is known as *Astrometeorology.* Both Electional Astrology and Astrometeorology were permitted by the Christian

Church throughout the sweeping suppressions of the late medieval period. These astrological uses were deemed compatible with God's intended uses of the stars as expressed in Genesis 1:14 (King James).

"And God said, Let there be lights in the firmament of the heaven to divide the day from the night; and let them be for signs, and for seasons, and for days, and years." Genesis 1:14

However, sometimes, *Electional Astrology* and *Astrometeorology* step on each other's toes, as is the case in this amusing true story!

Luciano and Carla were a lovely Italian couple. He was a broad backed sailor eager to start a family, and she a sophisticated paleontologist with raven tresses. They applied to me to select their perfect wedding date. Though commonplace in many parts of the world, this request is atypical in the U.S.A. Maybe I get one request every two to three years. I was happy to comply.

First, I asked them *"what activities do you wish to enhance in your marriage? Children, career, money, travel, romance, property?"*

Couples are different so you really must ask. Not everyone wants kids! Luciano and Carla agreed that they were homebodies and love bugs.

"We want children, a house, and a great domestic life," they said, exchanging warm glances. Clearly, they were in love.

Next, I had them give me a ball park of time in which to hunt. *"Summer through Fall this year,"* they decided.

"Can you marry any day of the week, at any time?"

Now don't laugh. For the sake of a happy home, the exact planetary alignment chosen might indicate that midnight is the best time to get married. The couple provided me their schedules, and also their city of choice.

"Give me a week to complete your commission," I said, after taking down their birth data. First, I calculated both of their natal charts, and then their "transits" and "progressions" for the time window of choice. First, I teased out several good looking dates within the six month period suggested. Then, the narrowing process began.

Because this couple requested fertility and property, I was alert for days showing an abundance of planetary energy in the water signs of Cancer, Pisces or Scorpio. *Why water signs?*

Water is the element of love! Water is the sexiest element. Water is domestic, receptive and romantic. Most of all, it's fertile! And yes, it's lucky for property. Water was also the most harmonious element between Luciano's and Karla's personal charts because they were both born in water signs! There was no doubt, water signs it must be.

I found a lovely date. A promising summer's day, in a predictably fair weathered of choice. Next, I set about to select the exact minute.

"An exact minute to marry?," you might be asking yourself. Why of course! We must remember that the beginning of a stone's throw marks its path.

As an aside, I am the first to admit a good marriage time does *not* make the marriage.

One might think of bride and groom together as representing a young tree that is about to be planted. This tree (the couple) already exists, but the soil is important too. The right time of marriage provides the best possible soil for this tree to flourish. If you think of the planetary weather as analogous to soil, it becomes easy to understand!

Sometimes you have a sickly tree but great soil. This will help the tree of marriage to "come around," but not always. At other times the reverse holds true - we have a strong and vital tree with lousy soil. The couple will soldier on, despite limiting conditions. A weak tree rooted in deficient soil will certainly fail. A strong tree planted in fertile soil will flourish!

I suppose the *Nuptial Horoscope* was ever so much stronger in the days when people met, married and consummated the union all within a few hours!

So, there I sat at my desk, finally having found the perfect minute, with an preponderance of water energy. Water, water everywhere.

The marriage was scheduled for a summer day. The loving ceremony would lead up to that specially timed magic moment where Luciano would place the ring on Carla's hand, and kiss the bride.

As the story goes, it rained during the ceremony. No, it poured. It poured so hard that some tables were overturned and the newlyweds fled indoors. However, happiness also rained upon the couple! Luciano and Carla immediately found their perfect home, and soon produced two beautiful children in quick succession. They reported domestic bliss and were extremely happy last we spoke.

One might see Luciano and Carla's water sign loaded "wedding date deluge" as mere coincidence if this sort of thing did not happen all the time in astrological practice! Although I regret the embarrassment of the marriage date downpour, I continue to arrange marriages with lots of water signs. Only now, I warn my couples to expect rain.

THE CAT WHO LOVED MUSIC

Twilight was born in a cardboard box on a lovely spring day in May in Oakland, California. A tiny black longhaired kitten with luminous gold eyes. Twilight grew into an exceptionally beautiful, rather large cat.

Fortunately for me, her thoughtful owner had documented the exact moment of Twilight's birth without dreaming that one day, Twilight's story would be memorialized here. Twilight the cat was a Taurus, born as Venus exactly rose in the east, in the sign of Gemini. Beautiful Venus, the planet of melody, governed her horoscope.

Traditionally, a woman born with this same chart would be beautiful, vain, chatty and most of all, an aficionado of melodious music, literature and culture. Although a cat, Twilight appeared to be all of these things. There was no doubt as to her beauty. Everyone would comment upon this simply gorgeous creature. And vain? She would sit patiently and poised upon her grooming perch, feet together, waiting to be brushed. She was an expressive conversationalist, not only adept at talking but also having a tendency to eagerly respond when addressed. Twilight enjoyed poetry readings, and strangely, raisins.

But most "Venusian" of all, was the most unusual interest and pleasure she took in fine music. She particularly loved the famous voice of the saturnine opera diva Maria Callas.

No sooner would a Maria Callas album begin playing than Twilight would lie upside down, head next to the speaker. She appeared to be in a rapturous state of trance. Stranger still, if while reclining I commenced singing melodious Irish "airs," Twilight would hurry to climb upon me and then, place her ear directly upon my vocal chords, as if to absorb the sound, purring loudly all the while.

When Twilight turned eighteen, her arthritis was so bad she would not incline to move about. She would sleep for hours in one place, as old cats do. However, when I took my black walnut folk harp out to play, Twilight displayed a remarkable interest. Hauling herself off the couch with painful difficulty, she would plant herself directly in front of the harp, fixing her eyes upon me in obvious anticipation of a personal concert.

Twilight understood the concept of intact songs, acknowledging each performance with the gesture of an outstretched paw, retracting her arm on commencement of each song. After four or five selections, she would clamber with difficulty back up onto the sofa. If I played a flute, she would quickly appear from anywhere in the large house and curl herself up in my lap. Yes, there was no doubt that this was a cat who loved music, as promised by the exact rising of Venus at the precise moment of her birth.

Twilight responded to Venus' vibrations just as strongly as might a human being born at the same time as she. Perhaps a cat is a person too?

THE TIME TRAVELERS

I am completely respectful of those readers who do not believe in reincarnation.

However, this story may be of significant interest to those that do. As a small child, I was plagued by memories of what appeared to be another life, so in my case, the relevance of past lives has never been in doubt. As a natural born scientist, I've researched the subject extensively and thus, was intrigued to receive an invitation to test my theories with a local "past life research group." To reiterate the *Preface*, I've changed names and other particulars to shield identities. However, the facts of the cases here are all true.

In the early 90s, I received an invitation from a local Northwest psychologist of high repute to test the validity of Astrology before his group of personal past life researchers. For weeks they had been engaging in deep hypnosis, ferreting out the details of their past lives. Because they shared their findings amongst themselves, most of the class members were well aware of each other's past life particulars long before I entered the scene. However, I knew nothing of their findings.

The plan was that I would draw class member's birth charts upon the blackboard, and then deduce from the planets the dominant details of their prominent past lives.

The room was full of eager eyes when I entered the small room. Being a much larger group then anticipated, I felt a bit unnerved. The door was closed and the shades were drawn. So why was Astrology on trial in a group of self admitted time travelers?

The idea was that if past lives were indeed true, then one's horoscope should be able to describe them, at least in a general way. And why should that be, you might well ask?

Prominent planetary patterns in the chart are not considered random. Rather, they reflect your own fields of previous focus. For instance, Mozart's proverbial childhood musical genius would be attributed to past lives investing himself in music. This investment of time and talent would be mirrored in his present horoscope through the prominence of the musical planets i.e., Venus, Neptune, Mars and the Moon (in combination).

The same rule would go for negative accomplishments. The great guru Paramhansa Yogananda reported that he almost dropped a baby someone had placed in his arms because he realized it had been a murderer in it's past life! Certainly, this infant was reborn with criminal tendencies that would show up again in his birth chart!

In this paradigm, it could be said that we are attracted to a birth time that best reflects us. Our horoscope then describes who we *already* were at birth, just as much as it shows our ongoing future potentials.

Please note that one needn't "believe" in past lives to practice Astrology. Many respected astrologers are exclusive advocates of the *Mono Life* (one life) theory. However, the reincarnationist can opt to view the natal chart through a reincarnation-inclusive paradigm.

So there we all were. I looked at the crowded class, and they stared back at me. Doctor Morris, who lead the group, volunteered to be our first test subject. I sketched his chart with chalk upon the board. What I saw astonished me. There, in the astrological "9th house" of religion, were the "malefic" planets, cruel Mars and cold Saturn, joined in fiery Aries. It didn't take long to decipher this.

"Maybe you were burned at the stake in your past life," I ventured.

To my not so great surprise, he agreed. Yes, he had been a burned at the stake in the era of the Salem witch trials. This was apparently common knowledge in the group as they had been discussing the very incident for weeks, long before I opened my mouth. They seemed pleased with the immediate clarity of their leader's birth chart.

The next candidate volunteered, a gentleman named Barry. His chart was drawn super size on the black board. With white chalk I rendered an entirely different chart then the former sample. Instead of Mars and Saturn being prominent, this horoscope was all Venus, Moon and Neptune!

"Wine, women, song and the sea," I mused, *"You might have been a sailor?"*

A assenting gasp rippled through the room. The group had already been discussing Barry's past life as a womanizing, drunken sailor for some time.

Next, a dark haired and morose woman stepped forth, offering her birth chart for testing. Unfortunately, I cannot remember what I saw or said, other than the fact that once again, we hit a bull's eye. Three out of three tested charts resulted in a one hundred percent exact match to the test subject's self description of a "known" and assumed past life. At first try.

Certainly, these methods are far from "scientific" and the qualified skeptic will cite many reasons to question our conclusions.

However, an intuitive pragmatist will find yet another confirmation in the powers of the astrological birth chart to see deeply into the mysteries of human life. The birth chart does seem to consistently perform as a wondrous telescope into the character, karma and destiny of man.

THE CALLING

We are all familiar by now with the ongoing debate amongst the psychologists between "nature" and "nurture." Psychologists tend to ask questions such as; *Are we the product of our genes or our environment? Is character inherited or created?* It seems obvious that both are true, with the balance vying between individuals. But what of a *third* factor? *What of the human soul?* This is neither genetics, nor culture. This innate soul-nature appears to be at last partially reflected in the arrangement of the cosmos during our first breath.

In my whole life of reading charts, I've encountered but three cases of charts that did not "fit" their owners. Later, it so turned out that all three of these "off" readings were for persons who had wrongly cited their birth times! Other astrologers have shared this same experience. After all, why would thousands of intelligent people worldwide continue with Astrology if it flat out didn't work? So we see a third factor is at work in human character. Mysterious, yes. But the ancients were no fools. This next story is a curious look at the phenomenon of what one might call *the planetary contribution.*

In the late 70s, I attended a number of colorful astrological lectures at the famous *Cody's Books* on Telegraph Avenue in Berkeley, California. So did Ed, a wild and wiry, black-haired carpenter whom if not for his drinking habits, could qualify for sainthood. He didn't eat meat, and spent most of his on and off time assisting the disabled. He wrote poetry and powerful stories of universal love. Here and again down the years we would meet and compare our life notes. He was always full of warm stories from his endless rambles; but whatever was said and done, the predominant fact of this man's life was his overwhelming devotion to a life of peace.

All the while, Ed was raising up his son Little Eddie Junior from a crisp, intelligent ten year old into a muscular high school graduate. Ed Senior liked Astrology. In fact, he liked it enough to try his hand at offering hand drawn horoscopes and readings at the famous local coffee houses. Little Eddie's chart was of considerable interest to us because it was overwhelmed by Mars, the God of War. Who would have thought? He was raised his whole life under the tutelage of a loving father who taught him the kindly ways of Venus. But there was no doubt about it, Little Eddie was a Martian. How would this play out in his oncoming adulthood?

Mars dominated this boy's birth chart by appearing on the eastern horizon at his birth, a place of considerable honor in the horoscope. Not only this, but Mars was in Scorpio, his "home" sign. In the old days, the astrologers would look toward the planets nearest the rising degree to describe the character of the child being born.

Any child born with Mars rising in his home sign was said to arrive with considerable fighting talent, courage, temper, energy and strength. It is the manner in which he/she chooses to use these powerful forces that is up to him. Its rather like being born with a nice big hammer in your hand. Would Little Eddie use this hammer to build a house or to hit himself over the head? So, here we had Eddie Junior, a child of Mars being born to Ed Senior, a natural son of Venus. Of course, we are all children of God, but we do have our individual planetary predilections. I pointed out Eddie Junior's dominating Mars to his father warning,

"Prepare yourself, because that son of yours will wish to follow the warlike ways of Mars."

These were not words a saint would want to hear. However, Ed Senior was philosophical about this news. A staunch "believer" in reincarnation, he realized that every soul cometh from afar, imbued with its own habits. The renowned American seer Edgar Cayce remarked that a child's birth chart shows us the greater "proclivities" or tendencies that he carries over from his own activities in past lives. This idea is in full agreement with the view of the *Jyotish* or Hindu astrologers of India. We are not blank slates at birth!

Certainly, Little Eddie's birth chart was that of a great warrior reborn!

However, Eddie Junior was still a child, and many years must yet pass until we could observe the fulfillment of his choices.

The day finally came when Little Eddie graduated from high school, shocking his Dad with an announcement that he had joined the U.S. Army. More so, he had specially requested to serve in infantry despite the many safer options available to someone with his technical skills. No, the infantry it must be! To compound matters, his dream job and future plan was to become a trained interrogator in the Mideast! This didn't surprise me, because I had been expecting something of this sort to unfold for years.

However, stunned upon hearing this discomforting news, Ed Senior shaved his head and immediately headed off for an isolated Zen Monastery.

But what was to be done? A warrior son was born to a man of peace. It was sealed in the stars. Or *was it?* Little Eddie's chart showed something else too! Mars, the dominant planet of war was closely joined to his "point of self-undoing." (This point describes where you are most prone to self-injury and spiritual backsliding). This point is also known as the *South Lunar Node*. One old interpretation for one born when Mars conjoins the South Lunar Node is this; *"anger, war and fighting will be his undoing."*

It seemed that the fighting life was not preordained after all, but was instead, a dangerous choice set before the lad! *So what might his positive choice be?* To discover this, we always look to the *opposite* point in the chart. This opposite point is called the *North Lunar Node*, indicating one's *dharma* or literally *"the work that is right for the soul to do."* In every chart these two Lunar Nodes are always placed exactly opposite to one another! Little Eddie's positive path was shown as opposite to the dominant position of his warring Mars joined to his "point of self-undoing." *And where then, might his rightful work be?* You guessed it, in the sign of Venus, the Bringer of Peace.

Astrology is a science in itself and contains an illuminating body of knowledge. It has taught me many things, and I am greatly indebted to it. Geophysical evidence reveals the power of the stars and the planets in relation to the terrestrial. In turn, Astrology reinforces this power to some extent. This is why Astrology is like a life-giving elixir for mankind.

Albert Einstein

Preface

While it could be said that being able to predict the future is a novel skill, I have found that this ability brings along with it many interesting challenges. Does Astrology itself inherently have the ability to predict the future? The answer to this question is:

Yes and No.

Astrology can at times be uncannily accurate at describing human behavior. This includes behaviors that have yet to happen. The reason for this is that Astrology is a study of how the sky and the stars get within us. How they affect us internally, through our emotions and by their magnetic urges. At times, life can in fact seem to take hold of us and lead us down certain trains of thinking. The pull of the celestial forces do seem to work in this manner. The moving planets mix with our inner being, our energetic "DNA," and we feel pulled and urged on through these mixings.

When we think about this fact logically, Astrology doesn't seem unrealistic at all. Our bodies are made from cells. Within each cell at any given time, there are many tiny processes occurring, and the sensitivity of these internal building blocks could quite easily be affected by the planetary movements.

In fact, I grew up with a father who is a well-known astrophysicist, having built the largest infrared telescope in the world on Jelm Mountain in Laramie, Wyoming. Yes, I grew up with a father who has made a career of measuring the infrared emissions from the planets and stars. From a very young age, I remember focusing the telescope, which sat like a monument under its large dome, reminiscent of R2D2 from Star Wars. When my brother and I would ride in the back seat of my dad's brown Chevy hatchback, we would see the large white dome on the horizon and yell, " R2D2!! " At the bottom of the peak, we would climb into huge orange Snocats and slowly grizzle up the mountain to the telescope. It was in this environment that I learned to exist, under the stars on the top of a mountain. When standing on a mountain, the vibration of the stars is a real phenomenon. The vault of stars is unendingly fluorescent without the false lights of the city masking its effects. The celestial vault can literally "take your breathe away."

My mother was not an astrophysicist. She is instead a genius in the area of human relationships. Having gotten her Masters degree in Psychology, my mom went on to work in a variety of human relations fields. She has done everything from managing a Family Planning clinic to working as a vocational rehabilitation counselor. She won the first car I ever drove through her work as a successful Mary Kay make-up sales woman[4]. My mom currently works doing high level fundraising for the libraries, a skill she must have learned while also being the mayor of our town for 12 years.

---

[4] A cream-colored Oldsmobile *Firenza*. The car came with a free "mix tape" in the stereo tape deck. Those were the days!

It is the marriage of the two temperaments of an astrophysicist and an intuitive diplomat that seem to have created a lifetime translator and Astrologer. The reason for the life story here is not so much personal, but is instead meant to illustrate the true gifts of Astrology. Astrology is a science that merges the magical vault of stars with the human psyche. Astrology could be said to be a study of the Astral Psyche.

In ancient Greece, Astrology was a school of thought that developed naturally along with Astronomy, Philosophy, and the other great studies. While each ancient astrologer naturally has a bit of their own style in thinking about the subject, the unifying theme of Astrology itself is that it has been an ancient study of the " logic and meaning of the stars. " The manner in which the stars affect our logical thinking. Our health. Our appetites. The manner in which the stars urge us on and pull at us. A very interesting study indeed!

Most of all, I would say that Astrology is a study of people. It is the study of human drives and human behavior. The astrological chart is a schematic diagram of the planets and sky at the moment of a person's birth. This map illustrates the celestial energy configuration at the time of that birth. The chart reflects our geometric inbeing, It influences the manner in which we experience the effects of the currently moving planets. In this way, the astrological chart is a map that is moving. The chart breathes.

It is the uncanny accuracy of every single astrological chart that keeps me interested in the study of Astrology.

The intricacy, exactness, and depth of Astrology is a true gift to the world!

The experience of knowing this art and science has been a comical addition to my personal relationships In the stories that follow, I invite you into my everyday life, so that you too can enjoy and be in awe of Astrology, as I continue to be each and every single day.

True Stories

Andrea L. Gehrz

The Skeptic

I am often asked if I get offended when people don't believe in Astrology. I answer this question by explaining that some charts do not lend themselves to a belief in Astrology, but are instead more attuned to other interests. In fact, I find that the occasional skeptic adds a bit of spice to my day!

I will never forget a particularly enthusiastic client by the name of Germain, as he arrived ready and eager to be skeptical about Astrology. Germain's partner was a massage therapist and had sent him for an Astrology reading so that he might learn a bit about the " spiritual side of life. " After a great reading with a large number of fascinating questions from the semi-open skeptic, we began to wrap up. At this point, I suddenly received an urging from the unseen realm, pushing me onwards to go ahead and make a future prediction.

Germain's soul seemed to be craving proof of the magical under-workings of life. There is nothing better than an accurately timed future prediction to spice up one's thinking! I looked into the chart to see what the planets might reveal. I noticed that in the month upcoming, a large number of planets would converge on Mr. Happy-Skeptic's *Saturn*.

Saturn is cold and constricting, and can often bring struggles into our lives. Saturn problems tend to be the kind that force us to grow and mature, and can often be accompanied by deprivation or the experience of having limitations put upon us. Depending on the condition of Saturn in the chart, these restrictions could manifest as anything from a pair of pants that ride up all day, to the common teenage Saturn experience of being "grounded."

The unseen forces were urging me strongly, so I went ahead and wrote down an exact date and time for Germain to watch in the future. I then began to lay out the details.

As I examined the upcoming events of Germain's life, I noticed that the planet of Saturn was sitting in the house of siblings and that it would soon be under the influence of the moving planets. This configuration indicated upcoming stress in regards to one of Germain's siblings.

I explained the kinds of things that might happen on the day that I had written down.

" *On this date you may experience some serious stress in relation to the siblings. This sibling stress could also in some way be connected to addiction and places of confinement, such as hospitals or jails. Oh and also driving.*"

The reading ended and Germain and I parted ways. As with any divinely-ordained future prediction, it was time to wait and see what might come to pass.

A few months later I received an email. It turns out that on the exact date I had predicted, the once skeptical Germain's sister had been picked up by the police while on tour with her band. She had been pulled over for drinking and driving, was presented with a DUI, and put in jail.

Astrology 1   Skeptics 0

Special Sauce

People often ask me what it's like to work as an astrologer. They enthusiastically inquire,

" *Do you ever see something really horrible coming in a chart? If so, what do you do?!*"

Or, " *Have you ever seen a relationship chart that was awful, and wanted to tell the people to break up?*"

The simplest answer to these questions is, " *Yes, I have seen charts that are hard to handle!*" The more complicated answer is that I make a very strong effort to never incidentally create a *bad future* by focusing on the challenging parts of an astrological chart. Instead, when I see something that might be a bit of a struggle, I attempt to provide clients with a number of ways to channel such energies in a more positive fashion.

In a more philosophical sense, it could be said that nothing in life is perfect, yet some charts are much easier to wrangle than others.

These questions remind me of a time when I sat down with a good friend and her newlywed husband for a *composite chart* reading. A *composite chart* indicates the evolution of energies that will occur during the melding of two people. We all have witnessed that certain couples age well over time, getting along better as the years go by, while others conjoin into the type of partnership that is inherently cold, or in which they tend to explosively argue or criticize one another.

As I sat looking at the composite chart of my friend and her newlywed husband, I was a bit perplexed at how these specific joint energies would express themselves over time. I saw great emotional happiness between the two of them; the kind of idealistic and emotional partnership that continues on throughout the years, growing into a long a fruitful relationship. The chart appeared sweet, tender, loving, and prolific in regards to children. At the point in time that I was examining the chart, the newlywed couple had already bore one child together, and another was on the way.

I acknowledged the sweetness that would be ever-present within this couple, yet at the same time my eyes arrived upon something in the chart that appeared to be quite harsh and unforgiving. The planet of Mars, which indicates the active life of a couple, was highly maltreated in this composite chart. Mars was harshly placed in the house of religious beliefs.

The ninth house in the chart is said to be connected with the human urge to expand one's thinking, which often occurs through a religion or some other sort of life philosophy. It appeared that this couple would merge into coldness and crankiness of the most intense kind in reference to religious differences.

As an astrologer, this is a calculation that can very easily be made. Mars is a hot planet, which makes sense in relation to passion. It gets riled up and makes people want to differentiate from those around them. The planet of Saturn is almost antithetical to the nature of Mars. Saturn is extremely cold. When these two planets mix in a composite chart, they can pose hard challenges in the life of the couple. Saturn will inherently cool off the passion projected by Mars. A composite Saturn/ Mars connection can lead to all sorts of blockages in a relationship. In the case of this particular couple, the blockages existed around religious beliefs.

Not only did this relationship have the aforementioned Mars/Saturn connection, the planet of Pluto was also joining these planets in their already challenging angular relationship to one another. The presence of Pluto added even more depth and power to the blockage.

As I sat considering the options at hand, I wondered just how to handle this very delicate information. I did not want to create harsh thinking about the relationship, nor did I want to omit any part of a true analysis.

After much contemplation, I decided to gently mention that the biggest challenge the couple could have might be in regards to belief systems, religious philosophies, etc. I mentioned the possible deep and intense cold energies that might emerge, while making sure to provide the couple with umpteen ways to deal with this problem, if it were in fact to ever come up.

One of my favorite things about the technique of analyzing composite charts is that they can describe very accurately the nature of a relationship and how it will emerge and evolve over time. It could very simply be said that each merging of two people creates its own " *special sauce.* " Some relationships are good for certain activities such as starting a business, while others are better for wanting to continually engage in the act of sharing common beliefs.

I will never forget the very interesting evolution of the mixing of these two people. Just as indicated by all of the goodness in the composite chart, this couple is still thriving and happy five years later! The family vibe is alive and well, and these two individuals exude feelings of warmth and mutual respect. This doesn't sound odd or even unusual for a married couple.

But these two are no longer married!

This couple is currently separated on account of the wife coming out as a Mennonite. The wife in this marriage had in the past thought about joining the Mennonites, but had never pursued this path wholeheartedly. At the exact time period in the composite chart in which the *religious differences* blockage was lit up by the traveling planets, the wife fully immersed herself in the Mennonite belief system. Irregardless of the religious beliefs of these two individuals, they are both still able to joyfully and gracefully co-parent and be good friends. Their energies have mixed in a way as to produce a true and idealistic love and they continue to discover wonderful ways to work through their religious differences, especially in respect to raising their children!

I often wonder why people don't routinely check the composite chart before settling down, as this is a very practical use of Astrology!

The Curiosity Disorder

When I was a young and innocent astrologer, I used to " jam out charts. " At least that is what my best friend used called it. He would say things like, " *You jam out charts, just like musicians jam out music. They go to parties and if music is playing, they just have to jam. That's how you are about doing charts. You just can't stop yourself!*"

And he was right. When someone asked me to look at their chart, I saw it as an exciting opportunity to learn something!

I now remember a time when I learned something very important while " jamming out " a chart. Astrology is very exact!

One day many years ago, I went to the local community college to work as a Sign Language interpreter. For long classes and challenging jobs, interpreters tend to work in teams so that we can keep our minds and arms fresh. One particularly fun assignment I received was to interpret an Auto Mechanics class. During the break, my team interpreter and I began to discuss Astrology. He asked questions about the art of astral study and my *curiosity disorder* began to bubble up as I pondered the specific details of his chart.

During a break from class, we excitedly snuck into the computer lab to pull up his details. We chatted about various aspects of the chart, heartily going back and forth about what all the planets and their angles meant, and what was happening in his life at the time.

As I observed the chart, I had a nagging feeling that it was somehow incorrect. As he talked about his current health situation, the chart became clearer before my eyes. According to the birth time provided, he should have been born with the sign of Gemini on the eastern horizon at the time of birth. Although the chart represented the birth time he had given me, he simply did not look like a Gemini rising!

Gemini risings tend to be thin and move quickly, and they often vibrate with a speedy and kinetic frequency. Mr. Team-Interpreter's energy was very earthy and his physical appearance, vibration, and actions seemed much more well-matched to a Capricorn rising.

I told him so.

I insisted, " *I don't think that this birth time is correct. Actually, let me just move the chart around a bit. There. That's better. Looks much more like you!* "

At the end of the day, we happily parted ways and I didn't think much of the tiny reading.

Years later, after interpreting a public event, I ended up in a conversation about Astrology with another colleague, someone who happened to be a mutual friend of the interpreter whose chart I had " jammed out," years earlier.

At one point in the conversation, the mutual friend began to enthusiastically question me. "*How did you do it?*" he inquired.

"*Do what?*" I inquired back.

He replied, "*I heard a story about you! A certain Capricorn rising told me how you looked at his chart a few years ago and said that you thought his birth time might be wrong. And you were right! He said that he went home and found his birth certificate, and he was a Capricorn rising. How did you do that?!?*"

To this I responded, "*It's easy to find the correct birth time because people look like their charts! And they vibrate like them!*"

The Ossified Man

People often ask me how I became an astrologer. The simplest answer is that it is " in my chart " to be an astrologer! On a more complex level, I would say that Astrology provides an unending outlet for my intense curiosity. The reason for this is that Astrology is a study of people and each person is so very different.

Every now and again, I get obsessed with a certain astrological topic. When I say obsessed, I mean the kind of fixation that does not subside until I learn everything I possibly can about that very subject.

Many years ago, I took an interest in the charts of circus performers. I became enamored with the charts of people with unique bodies, as people tend to look like their charts. Quite often, special bodies correlate to very interesting charts!

I put on my headphones and set out to the library to peruse the *Guinness Book of World Records*. As I flipped through the pages, I happened upon the life story of the " Ossified Man. " Ossification is a process of hardening. Visual images of The "Ossified Man" showed him laying with his arms and legs jutting straight forward in an entirely unbending fashion. He looked as if his entire body was made of stone, wood, or some other hard substance.

I googled the " Ossified Man " to see if I could find his date of birth. By some stroke of luck, I was able to locate his biography, chock full of pertinent information, conveniently including the finer details of his birth. I promptly went to my *Ephemeris* in order to draw up the chart of this exceptionally bony fellow.

The *Ephemeris* is the most important astrological book in existence, as it is the book that holds within it the tables indicating where all the planets are on any given day.

I thumbed quickly back in time to the 1950s, as this was a period when it was still politically correct to celebrate *freakery*.

When I arrived at the date on which the "Ossified Man" came into the world so many years ago, I almost jumped out of my chair in a sudden and profound state of *astrological awe. Astrological awe* is the phenomenon of being awestruck by the surprising accuracy of Astrology. I still have this experience often after ten years in the field.

The Sun in the astrological chart is connected to the general state of the physical body and the way in which a person moves through the world. In this particular case, I could not believe my eyes!

The "Ossified Man" had been born on a very special yet very constricted day. Not only did he have his Sun sitting in the hard and bony sign of Capricorn but he had also been born with the cold and constrictive planet of Saturn exactly upon his Sun.

In medical Astrology, Capricorn is the sign that is said to rule the bones, as well as bony growths and substances. Depending upon the chart, bony growths could show up as bunions, bone spurs, or other ailments that affect the hard structures of the body.

Here in the chart of the " Ossified Man, " who could be said to have been the boniest of all bony individuals, was the boniest and most constrictive configuration I had ever seen in an astrological chart!

The Sun in Capricorn suggests that the " Ossified Man " might have a manner of movement that is a bit constricted or contained. Saturn, the cold and constrictive planet, was also in the cold and constrictive sign of Capricorn. This condition can make Saturn even colder and more constrictive than usual. Saturn upon the Sun had obviously cooled off his body so much that it had hardened into the boniest of all bodies!

Albeit an oppressed science, Astrology is extremely accurate on many many levels! As a good astrologer friend of mine likes to say, " *You can't even make this stuff up!*"

Case Closed

Most astrologers have had the experience of looking at a chart, only to feel blocked from the information lying within it. While this has happened to me a few times throughout my career, I will never forget one particularly important lesson I learned about this exact experience.

I once attended a lecture at an Astrology conference, in regards to using the " best practices " as a professional astrologer. The astrologer giving the talk had suggested that it was not a good idea to see clients more often than once or twice a year. The lecturing astrologer was of the opinion that more frequent readings might make the client overly dependent on astrological insight. Respecting and understanding the spirit behind this approach, I adopted a bit of the same philosophy in my own practice.

In general, this rule has served its purpose, but of course there are always exceptions to any rule. Such special cases are often divinely ordained. I learned this very important lesson from a certain family in distress.

The Jamila family had come into a tense situation regarding another family on their block. The neighbors of the Jamila family were suing them over a situation between the young children in both households. As the court proceedings moved along, uncle Jamila and grandmother Jamila found solace in the information that Astrology could provide, and had asked to come back for a consultation once every few months.

While I would normally encourage a family such as this to wait a while longer before coming in for another reading, this case seemed to be an exception. With every ounce of my being, I felt that I should see them again in two months, just as they had requested.

Each time they came for an update, the astrological information flooded through me, as would certain urgings from the divine and upper realms. I predicted correctly the month that their young child would be uprooted from her current circumstances, as well as a myriad of other happenings in regards the situation at hand.

It must be understood that these were not *willy nilly* predictions made for the fun of it. Each one was made after careful thought and very strong, persistent urgings from somewhere high up in the universe.

Then something very interesting happened!

The sticky situation was coming to an end and the Jamila family had decided to move across town to separate from the wily neighbors. At this point, I had seen the uncle and grandmother about three times and the information given thus far had been very useful to them. However, their last visit was very different.

I looked at the charts, yet I could not see anything! I could of course see all the planets sitting in the charts, but they appeared lifeless. Looking at them did not cause any images or information to appear in my mind's eye.

As I sat examining the charts, I said to the uncle and the grandmother, "*You know, I don't see anything! It is as if the story has come to an end. There is no need to make another appointment, because there is nothing more to say in regards to this matter!*"

And that was that.

It was through this experience that I learned a very important lesson in reference to the astrological and divine arts. A correct and healing future prediction does not come from the astrologer per se, but is instead a divinely ordained piece of information, set to be revealed only when the time is ripe.

The Tiny Nook

As an *astro-mama*, it can be nerve-wracking to know that your child might be approaching a period of planetary duress. People often ask me how I handle seeing such futures. The most honest response is, " *I watch and learn!*"

During my first few years as a mother, I worried quite a bit more than I do now. I have since witnessed the brilliance of children in naturally understanding how to handle their own energies. I remember a time when my daughter was 3 years old and I was out of town for work. I happened to take a glance at the *Ephemeris* and noticed that my little cutie had some challenging energies soon to hit her natal Saturn.

In adults, Saturn can express itself through limitations of all kinds, such as being strapped for cash, getting dumped, or being otherwise cut off from the things we want. In children and babies, Saturn often expresses itself as a need for limitation through structure and boundaries. In fact, children will often express Saturn energies by pushing boundaries in order to find out where certain structures exist, asking themselves questions such as:

"Is the cookie jar really off limits, or is this a soft boundary?"

"What happens if I step over the line at the bus stop?"

"Will every adult yell at me about this rule or only my mom?"

From the time my daughter was born, her dad and I would honor her Saturn periods by confining her through swaddling or by wearing her in a wrap. In these situations, a baby can learn happiness within confinement, as the limited movement becomes associated with the loving heartbeat of life.

Now that my daughter was 3 years old, I couldn't wear her in a wrap during her Saturn periods! So here, I had a problem. How could I *swaddle* her now that she was getting bigger?

On this particular occasion, I had gone out of town for a few Astrology lectures and I missed my little girl. It was as I checked the *Ephemeris* in preparation for clients, that I noticed my daughter's maltreated Saturn. I sat in my hotel room feeling a bit helpless. I wondered if she were feeling cut off from me and how I might help her handle these feelings in my absence.

Maybe she was feeling deprived in some other way?

I pondered what I might do for my girl during this potentially sad time. I chose a lesson in *mama restraint* and left her and her dad alone to fend for themselves. That night, while checking my email, I was delighted to see that I had received a message from her dad. I opened it and saw a picture of my baby girl, who had shoved herself in a tiny little nook in order to go to sleep that night.

Her dad told me that she had emphatically stated,

"Dad, I am sad. I am going to build myself a tiny nook and I am going to sleep in it. Then I won't feel so sad."

While I will never know if my daughter learned this behavior from her experiences being swaddled as a tiny baby, I do know that her actions tend to match up uncannily with her astrological chart, nearly every single time!   In this case, she had swaddled herself in a tiny enclosed space, which was a natural way for her to be confined into a feeling of safety and calmness. Being separated from others physically is a great use of Saturn!

As an *astro-mama,* I am more than happy to know that my daughter is already learning how to be find joy within the confinements of earthly life!

Night Shift

My many years of working as a Sign Language interpreter have never, ever been boring. In fact, I funded my most recent written translation through a very interesting night job as a " Video Remote Sign Language Interpreter. " At this particular job, I worked from home navigating emergency room visits for people via video conferencing technology.

As an astrologer, this job was very juicy!

Each night during the twilight hours, I sat in my upstairs office with a headset on, connected to hospitals around the country. During these late night shifts, there would be long periods of silence interrupted by sudden bursts of calls. And thus, I would frequently notice trends.

Now mind you, these trends were not something that I was making up, nor am I exaggerating.

They were so apparent that I would often get on *instant messaging* with the interpreter who had worked the shift prior to mine and she would ask me questions such as,

" *Is there a Full Moon? Is Mercury in Retrograde? Something weird is going on!*"

Or, "*Oh my goodness! What is going on with the planets? I had four cases of appendicitis in one shift!*"

How does this work? Medical Astrology can be quite simple. When studying the physical body according to the chart, each astrological sign is said to represent certain parts of the body. Now, imagine if the whole circle of the zodiac were to be clipped at the point between the signs of Aries and Pisces. This circle of signs could then be laid out in a straight line and placed next to a drawing of a human being.

If we were to do this exercise, we would notice that the sign of Aries represents the top of the head while the sign of Taurus rules the ears, nose and throat. Gemini is connected with the arms and fingers, and the sign of Cancer rules the chest and the pleura around the lungs. As we can see, the signs move right down the body in exact order, continuing downwards until arriving at Pisces, the sign which rules the feet.

In medical Astrology, each planet brings a certain energy to the part of the body indicated by the sign in which it is placed. For instance, the planet of Saturn constricts things, causing coldness and suppression to the part or parts of the body indicated by its sign. Here is a simple example.

Saturn in Aries: *Suppression/ Constriction in the Head*

Health manifestations: *Migraines, eye squinting, tight feelings in the head or scalp, etc.*

I will never forget the day that the Moon walked up to the exact same place as Saturn during one of these nighttime emergency room shifts. On this particular evening, Saturn was situated in the sign of Libra. The sign of Libra is said to rule the Kidneys. The Moon also being in Libra would indicate that its emissions were being focused into the area of the kidneys. The Moon herself is said to rule the internal fluids, and she thus contributes to the physical and emotional states of the masses. We have all heard about how emergency rooms and psych wards become very busy under the influence of the full moon and eclipses!

As I sat in my station, I looked in the *Ephemeris* only to notice that the Moon had just walked up to sit on top of Saturn. The calls began to pour in. I quickly noticed an obvious trend:

Kidney Suppression & Kidney Failure!

Within one hour, I had interpreted three separate cases of suppressed kidney function, for three different patients, in three different cities!

In fact, I had never interpreted this complaint before and I have not interpreted it since that night. What is even more interesting is that one of the three patients had already been in the hospital for a few days. On this very evening, his test scores had unexpectedly indicated severely oppressed kidney function!

As mentioned, these trends would show up often during my nighttime shifts and were quite pronounced. I distinctly recall another day at this job when three planets had come into a particularly wily and gross combination.

The Sun, Pluto, and Mars had converged into a few very strong angles to one another. Pluto tends to bring intense health problems, the kind of diseases that might force a person to consider topics such as *death and rebirth*. In extreme cases, Plutonian problems can show up in the form of flesh-eating diseases, eating disorders, auto-immune problems, etc. Mars brings inflammation and surgery, while the Sun rules the physical constitution itself.

Now let us recap: *Intense flesh-eating energies + inflammation + the entire physical constitution = ???*

On this particular evening, as the planets were mixing up this stew of flesh-eating and inflammatory vibrations, the Moon was walking up to trigger the whole configuration. Soon the calls started flying in. For one night and one night only, I began to interpret emergency room visits for gangrenous feet! The first call was from an old lady with diabetes. Her foot had begun to deteriorate from the bottom. Next came a call from a hiker who had been bitten by a snake a week earlier. The bite had begun to spread, causing red lines to travel up her otherwise healthy foot. I can't even remember the third caller, except for the obvious foot problem that I *do* in fact remember!

Of course, modern medicine was able to help all three of these patients through the use of antibiotics and surgery (which can be a great remedy in certain cases), but the astrologer in me would never be the same. In cases such as these, we see great proof of the accuracy of *Cosmic Biology*!

The Monsoon

People often ask me, " *Do you ever see something stressful coming in your own chart and if so, what do you do?"*

This story harkens me back to a time when I saw a particularly stressful alignment approaching, and the seemingly fated fate that ensued.

During the final months of my pregnancy, my baby's father and I decided that our little girl needed a home. The astrologer in me was a bit nervous on account of the upcoming planetary stress to both her Dad's natal Moon and my own. This double occurrence of *Moon stress* surely indicated that there could be some upcoming distress in the home.

The Moon in the astrological chart is in part connected with the ability to be nurtured, cozy, fed, nourished, and protected. The Moon can also be connected with a person's physical house, since this is the location where we naturally feel at home and tend to get our basic, sustenance needs satisfied. When the Moon in an astrological chart is under planetary duress, there can be problems with the physical structure of one's house. The reason for this is quite simple. A stressful home life will inherently challenge and test the emotional needs of a person. Most simply put, it is very hard to feel calm and cared for when there is stress at home.

As a future *astro-mama*, this situation was perplexing. The astrologer in me thought on and on.

"Should we go ahead and buy a house under the planetary stress? I can't very well wait to buy a house when the realistic time is now! Maybe the Moon stress will simply manifest as the stress of taking care of a tiny baby."

As I hate to live in fear, we went ahead and purchased a house, which had been fully renovated with new windows and a new roof. Making sure to attend to all the important Saturn (structural) details, we hired the top inspector we could find. The house inspector turned out to be an interesting character, appearing thorough and skilled as he checked every tiny nook and cranny of the property. After he gave us the go ahead, we promptly completed the process of buying our new home.

On account of the fact that I was very pregnant, the double *Moon stress* still made me a bit nervous. While I sincerely hoped that this would manifest through intense caretaking, I could not shake my years of experience as a professional astrologer. As I prepared to give birth, I knew that *something* stressful was most likely in our near future, as two Moons in distress are much worse than one!

A month or so after moving into our new home, the Portland rainy season began. On the night of our last birthing class, future-daddy and I drove home through a thick shield of rain. We finally arrived tired and spent, excited to be in our cozy new home.

We put the key in the door and opened it. To our horror, it was not only raining outside but also in our living room! Throughout the room, water was dripping from the ceiling and running down the walls. The paint and plaster were sagging and weeping onto the floor, as water dribbled out of tiny holes throughout the entire ceiling.

The pregnant mother in me was horrified! The astrologer in me was mildly amused, as this occurrence was astrologically *right on the money.*

That night as I slept in the dry basement, the image of my unborn daughter appeared in my dream. She said, " *Mommy I want to come out now!* " My dream-self quite practically told her, " *Can you wait until Monday? The roof is collapsing.*"

That Monday morning at 8:00 am, I gave birth to my gorgeous daughter, at the same exact time that our new roof was being put on the house.

The Puppet

While I now choose to practice the intense art of *Radical Free Will*, there have been many times during my life as an astrologer that I have in fact doubted the existence of *Free Will* entirely. This story illustrates one of those moments.

Years ago, as I was preparing to leave my house for a Sign Language interpreting assignment, I opened up the *Ephemeris* to check my astrological weather for the day.

As my eyes moved down the page, they stopped upon both Mars and the Moon. The astrologer in me instantly took notice. You see, both Mars and the Moon were shining their beams upon my Mercury. In any chart, Mercury is the planet that indicates communication. While my Mercury is quite happy most of the time, the moving planets on this particular day were bringing in quite a bit of stress!

Mars and the Moon in this configuration suggested that the communications of the day would most likely be very heated and highly emotional in nature.

As I grabbed my coat and left the house, my mind began to roll over a number of different scenarios. Quite often, I have seen combinations of these three planets lead to fights. Even the simple combination of Mars and Mercury together can lead to verbal altercations, crankiness, and dissension of various kinds.

I thought to myself, " *Who on earth could I get in a fight with at work? I'm not the kind of person to fight with a client at work!*"

I sincerely hoped that the planetary configurations would be "wrong" or would somehow not affect me, as the last thing I wanted was a fight with an innocent co-worker. Yet as a freelance interpreter, I never quite know what to expect.

On this particular day, I was on my way to an "Adult Community Education" class. These kinds of jobs had always been very relaxed. After a half hour of driving, I arrived at the job and took my seat. I located the three Deaf students, who were all sitting at the same table, happily chatting and carrying on. We said our visual hellos and class began. Today's lesson was on English Grammar.

As the lecture portion of class was wrapping up, the teacher gave out an assignment. Having at this point forgotten about the planetary influences, I was taken off guard when I noticed a bustle over at the table where the Deaf students were sitting. One of them had taken offense to something the teacher had said and was fervently venting to the other two students at the table.

It was in this moment that I realized the manifestation of my seemingly fated astrological configuration. The angry Deaf woman waved me over so that she could give the teacher a "piece of her mind." I spent the next 15 minutes interpreting rude comments, insults, and

144

degrading remarks, straight from the hands of the Deaf student, right through my own mouth. I felt bad for the flummoxed teacher, yet delightfully shocked by the unending accuracy of Astrology.

As the student continued on, she became more and more riled up and was eventually asked to leave the class.

As I interpreted the angry remarks, I remembered the configuration of the planets. And appropriately so, I began to sincerely doubt the existence of *Free Will*. It is situations like this one that keep me interested in Astrology. The energies are entirely too magical and accurate to ignore!

Charmed

It could be said that Astrology is a true and complete study of humanity, inasmuch as it can explore every part of the human experience. I remember vividly a neighbor of mine who came in for a reading years ago. After looking at her chart, it became obvious that the upcoming year was going to be quite exciting in regards to tiny, lucky omens. Having just ended a messy divorce, my client was looking for some hope. Surprisingly, the energy flowing through her was electric and exciting! This lucky and optimistic part of her was going be turned on for the next few months.

After being prodded by the universe, I wrote down some upcoming dates. All of them were time periods in which her excited and hopeful self would be vibrating in full effect. I predicted luck of a very tangible kind. I saw four leaf clovers. Lots of them! While this seemed a bit frivolous to me, I could not shake the intense feeling that I was supposed to tell my client about them.

She mentioned that she had recently been noticing four leaf clovers and had found one just the other day. Again, I saw a large number of these lucky clovers flooding into my mind and felt compelled to write down a few more dates, on which my client might find more four leaf clovers!   ❧

While these predictions did not seem to make much sense, it turns out that they did come true nonetheless. Six times, all on the dates that I had written down! One of the magical clovers was found in the pouring rain, one was found under a rock, and several were spotted from the corner of her eye.

While it could be suspected that she had looked very hard for these clovers on the days I had written down, my client reported that she had put the dates away on purpose, making a point not to look at them. Each time that she spotted and picked a four leaf clover, she would go back and look at the dates and each time, she was shocked and amazed! The timing had been exact. She had discovered four leaf clovers on all of the dates listed!

The Strange Request

At times, parenting can feel like being the personal assistant to one's very own child. And thus, parents can at times unknowingly become ambassadors for needs that exist within the charts of their children. I remember vividly the moment when I learned this lesson.

A long time client had come in for reading. As we discussed her family, she mentioned something interesting about her four year old daughter Sarah. She explained Sarah's newest interest in detail stating, " *Sarah is so precious and tiny, yet she says that she really wants to get stopped over by the cops! She keeps bringing it up and obsessing about the time I got pulled over in Alabama.*"

Being a curious and diligent scientist of the soul, I looked into Sarah's chart. It was very obvious what was going on with my client's daughter. It turned out that little Sarah's chart was being highlighted in relation to authority figures! Her soul was looking to have a real and intense experience involving the enforcement of rules and regulations.

In Astrology, the planet of Saturn is said to rule the *fates of ignorance*; the things that we must learn through experience. In the case of Sarah's chart, her Saturn was in a very public and prominent position, and a few of the moving planets were turning this part of Sarah on like a light bulb! She was very much wanting to learn about the enforcement of rules and structures.

I relayed this to her mother and mentioned that it might be worth being " on the safe side, " as perhaps Sarah's soul might be needing a karmic brush with the law.

A few weeks later I got a call from Sarah's mother. She was very excited to relay the weekend's events to me, as little Sarah had indeed gotten stopped over! It turns out that just when the astrological timing was right, Sarah and her dad had been cruising around a river in their tiny motorboat, when they got pulled over by the Coast Guard.

In all of their years owning a house on a river, Sarah's parents had never had a brush with the law. This time however, the Coast Guard had noticed that they were driving with expired boat tags and the family river cruise was cut short. Sarah's mother said that when Sarah and her father returned to land, she had a most satisfied look on her face.

"Mom! Mom! I finally got stopped over!"
said Sarah, *"I knew I was gonna get stopped over!"*

Sarah's mom wanted to know if she or her husband might get pulled over again. She was hoping that Sarah's need to be chased by the police was coming to an end. I glanced in the *Ephemeris* and assured her that yes, Sarah's brush with the law had come right on time. The family was now in the clear!

Astral Gas

Over the years, I have seen many clients come and go. Most people only come to an astrologer once or twice in the span of their entire life. However, there have been a few clients that were unforgettable, and Diedre is one of them. I have never before nor since, had a client that I would go so far as to say was *extremely flatulent*.

The Ascendant Sign is very important in the chart. It is the sign rising on the eastern horizon at birth, and tends to greatly influence the personality. The rising sign also colors the manner in which an individual interacts with nearly everyone they encounter. The sign of Scorpio rules the colon and can be associated with the expelling of toxins, and the seedy underbelly of life in general. Scorpio can also at times make me think of swamps. It is the water sign that is connected with depth and intensity, just like the odors that might waft up from a swampy wetland.

When a person is born with planets sitting upon the Ascendant of the chart, these planets become very prominent in the expression of their personality. Planets that are rising up in the eastern horizon at the moment of birth create individuals who strongly represent the energetic quality of those planets. I remember the chart of this excessively flatulent client vividly. It looked extreme!

Diedre had been born at a moment when the planets of Mars and Uranus were sitting on top of one another.

This *conjunction* between Mars and Uranus was also rising up right near her Ascendant. In other words, Diedre was born at a time when Mars and Uranus were in the sign of Scorpio, which was rising up on the eastern horizon at the moment she was born.

Mars brings aggressive energies to the life, while Uranus brings electrical impulses. The fact that Diedre has these two planets exactly on top of one another means that she can at times get aggressively riled up and electric!

We must remember that in Astrology, the sign shows the manner in which the energies of the planets will be expressed. In this case, the electrical and aggressive tendencies were coming out very vibrantly because of their prominent placement in the chart.

As we sat together, I waxed on about the various parts of Diedre's astrological chart. Diedre, on the other hand, happily expressed her intense Scorpio energies by farting out lead repeatedly during the reading. She was in fact, excited by her own antics, as the rebellious energies welled up within her again and again. After Diedre had farted many times, I attempted to address the behavior.

Being the diligent professional that I am, I put on my most nonjudgemental lens. I said to Diedre, " *Exactly! Now this is just what I mean by having electric energies that want to be expressed through the more seedy parts of life! Unabashed and loud public farting is very Mars/ Uranus in Scorpio!*"

Tongue Tied

It is a true delight to have a happy and precocious couple in my office. I specifically remember a couple who felt like they were very much meant to be together. In fact, a series of *love omens* had kept them optimistic even though they could not seem to communicate all that well. For instance, their dads both happened to have the same middle names and their cats were born on the same day. While I can't remember all the details of their special connection, I will never forget the sweet and pure love they seemed to have for one another.

As I began to analyze their compatibility in relation to the planets, I noticed something quite striking. One of these girls had been born with an intense planetary combination in relation to communication blockages. The planet of Mercury is the planet that represents the urge to communicate and express one's needs. This girl had been born with the cold and blocking planet of Saturn directly upon her Mercury. I asked the couple a series of questions:

"Have you both been successful communicators in past relationships?"

"Are there days that you can communicate, and other days during which it is much harder to communicate?"

"Is one of you more expressive in general than the other?"

Through these questions, I learned a great deal about what might be contributing to the communication problem. The Mercury/Saturn partner had a hard time communicating her needs in nearly every aspect of her life, while the other partner seemed have an easier time talking about her feelings.

I then looked into the composite chart, as this would reveal what personality traits the two women would bring out in one another. I saw clear and free communication between the two women! I could see that the relationship itself could in fact remedy the communication struggles that the one girl had endured her entire life. I explained the benefits of the two women staying together, saying something to effect of:

" *I know that right now it seems like there are communication problems between the two of you. This is actually not a problem with the relationship itself. Instead, these moments of stress can be used to clear out old communication struggles of all kinds. I suggest that on the days that the two of you cannot seem to communicate, it might be best to remain silent with one another. Or perhaps you could slow down the communication by writing letters or only sending picture messages on your cell phones. If you can change the entire structure of the communications, this might help a great deal!*"

This sweet couple left happy and ready to try anything. I saw them again a few years later and they had gotten married. At this point in the relationship, they could talk about anything! In fact, the one who had been communicatively blocked mentioned that she had never felt more free to communicate than she does now. As Astrology continues to teach me every single day, it is not necessarily bad to struggle in relationships. It is instead important to make sure we are struggling to become better people.

Insatiable

Being the mother of a tiny baby can be quite distressing in general. This stress worsens when something is wrong with one's child but the source of distress is not obvious. I once received a call from the very tired mother of a five month old baby.

" *I don't know what is wrong! I feel like such a horrible mother! I have been feeding little Samantha all day and she still seems so irritable and frustrated. I am becoming tired and sore! Does her chart say anything about what could be wrong?"*

As we chatted, I reassured the very tired mother that I could almost certainly find the root of the problem in Samantha's birth chart, and that I would call her back after doing a few calculations.

As I drew up little Samantha's chart, I noticed something very interesting! Her Moon was being activated by many moving planets at the same time. The Moon in the astrological chart is the planet of the appetites, as well as the energy within us that needs to be nourished.

The problem with Samantha was very simple. She was going through a tremendous growth spurt! In fact, it seemed that for the next three days, this little girl would require a great deal more food than she had needed up until this point. Her poor mother couldn't keep up with her newly emerging appetite, as this little baby was preparing for a growth spurt of epic proportions.

I examined Samantha's Moon a bit further to see what kind of formula or milk-supplement would best be digested by her little body. I noticed that her Moon was in Virgo, which can tend to gravitate towards foods that are simple and clean.

I called Samantha's mother and we began to suss out the situation. I proceeded to ask her a few questions.

"Has Samantha ever done this before?"
"Does she seem genuinely famished to you?"
"Have you tried to feed her any solid food yet?"

As we discussed options, the mother mentioned that she was trying to wait until Samantha was six months old to give her any solid food, as this was what the parenting books had suggested.

I explained to the tired mother that Samantha was extremely hungry and that her simple tastes might respond quite well to some very basic rice cereal. I emphasized that for the next three days, Samantha would be experiencing a level of hunger that could surely surpass any she had experienced thus far in her short life. I reassured mama that she had done nothing wrong. Her baby was just growing rapidly!

A few weeks later I received a call. It turns out that Samantha was indeed ready for solid food. After being fed a tiny cup of rice cereal, she happily fell asleep. Since then, the mother says she can " feel it " when Samantha is going through another one of her expansive growth spurts.

Deja Vu

Once in a great while, a chart will show up in my office that seems uncannily familiar. In fact, sometimes a client will have a chart that is incredibly similar to that of a person I know quite well. This story is about a man who had been sent to my office by his wife, who herself happened to be a psychic. She had sent her husband to me for a reading, as she thought that Astrology might be scientific enough to appeal to his practical mind.

When I looked at Mr. Husbands chart, I recognized it immediately. I had watched this chart for years now. The father of my baby had almost the *exact* same chart! The two men were born within 6 hours of one another. While a true *astro-twin* is a person who is born on the exact same date and time as another person, these two were pretty darn close!

Two people who have incarnated within 6 hours from one another will be quite similar on a number of levels. The angles between all of the planets will be quite the same. The signs that the planets are sitting in will also be exactly the same. This means that the energies being expressed in the two lives will be almost identical. But because of the six hour difference between these two births, the energies of the two men would be expressed in different areas of the life. This might mean that they would not initially seem all that similar, but would have a flow of life-forces that was almost like that of identical twins.

The sign that is rising on the Eastern horizon at the moment of a person's birth is the sign that we astrologers call *the rising sign* or *the Ascendant*. Each sign of the zodiac tends to rise in a time period of approximately 2 hours. And thus, two births that have occurred in the same day, but 6 hours apart, will have the same planetary configuration but a different sign upon the *Ascendant*.

The *rising sign* becomes the sign that sits upon the first house of the chart. The next sign in zodiacal order will then rest upon the second house, and so on and so forth. In this case, the energies in the chart were being expressed in different areas of life for each individual. This could be likened to two songs being played with all of the same chords, but to two different audiences, in two different venues.

Having noticed the similarities in the charts, I became curious and excited to meet the psychic's husband. When he arrived, we immediately began to chat. By the time the reading was over, I had noticed many uncanny similarities between the two charts.

Both men had produced one child. Both of them with a certified psychic healer! One worked as an architect and a photographer. The other worked as an architectural photographer. They both buy, maintain and repair old cars. And they both are physically quite lean, even though this is not the norm in terms of their family genetics. It is times like this when I cannot believe that Astrology is not widely recognized for its astonishing insights into nearly every aspect of human life.

The Gay Spirit Guide

As an astrologer, I have had an extremely varied and interesting range of experiences. At times, a client will come into my office under the influence of Neptune. Neptune can bring about experiences that teeter on the *what is real and what is not*" continuum.

Many situations in life can bring about feelings of confusion, such as being lied to by someone we love, or through the researching of phenomena such as UFOs and aliens. Neptune can also be attributed to elusive health problems, such as rare disorders that are hard to identify, bizarre rashes, or weird aches and pains that may or may not be caused by food allergies.

On the particular day in question, it became apparent that my client was in fact needing some assistance with Neptune. It must be mentioned here that " astrologer " is *not* synonymous with " psychic. " In fact, many astrologers scoff at the idea of being psychic, as overly *woo-woo* practices are thought to dirty the scientific field of Astrology with charlatanism and fraudulent claims.

Nevertheless, Neptune persists in the chart and at times can express itself through interactions with the unseen realm. This could come in the form of seeing orbs, ghosts, or through disturbing dreams, premonitions, etc.

As the Astrology reading was coming to an end, the very calm and quiet suburban mom-looking client looked into my eyes and asked a question that could not quite be answered by the chart. She said, " *Can you tell me who my spirit guide is*?"

No sooner had she asked the question than the pictures began flooding into the section of air that floats in front of my psychic eye, located to the front and right of my actual right eye. At this young age, I would get quite anxious as the psychic messages flowed in, not yet quite understanding the breadth and depth of my own abilities.

I began to see a picture that seemed unfathomable. I timidly described what I saw, as the whole thing seemed altogether absurd to me.

"I see a man. He is sitting in one of those leather arm chairs. You know, the kind with all of those brass upholstery nails up and down the sides? He looks like an effeminate gay man, to be honest. And he has slicked down black hair with a long cigarette holder, and he is smoking a fancy cigarette."

Needless to say, the scientist in me was horrified. What kind of divine message was this nonsense? I looked at my client, only to see a tear of happiness fall down her cheek. She remarked, " *I have always wondered who that guy was! I am so glad I know now that he is my spirit guide!*"

I sat there, mouth agape. Could this really be true? Could someone's spirit guide really be a fancy gay man? It turns out that my client had been wondering who this fancy gay man really was for quite some time. Years earlier, a psychic from San Francisco had described the exact same man to this client but couldn't tell her who he was. Thankfully, my client's astrological chart had allowed her a moment of clarity into the Neptunian struggle of "what is real and what is not."

The Easter Man

People often ask me, " *How soon after a newborn baby arrives will their chart begin to emerge?* " Having watched the growth and development of my own daughter, I now enthusiastically reply, *"right away!"*

One of my favorite parts of this work is consulting with the parents of young children. Through Astrology, I attempt to provide parents with the most useful and positive language for their child's vibrations, no matter how odd they might be. In other words, I avoid *labeling language* at all costs, as this sets up the idea that the child might in some way be deficient or *less than optimal*. Instead, it is my goal to provide good uses for any sort of vibration that a child might naturally emit.

Do I think that the course of a child's life is entirely fated? The simplest answer is, " *No.* " The chart itself could be likened to a map of the child's temperament. The chart can help to shed some light on questions such as, " *Will she be an extreme extrovert or a shy poet?* " Or, " *Does she have a natural tendency to focus or would her mind be better used to invent new ideas and systems?*"

There are times, however, in which there is a huge amount of positivity in a child's chart. These are fun cases for the working astrologer!

I will never forget the chart of a certain little client named Lorna, whose father came into my office to hear about her natural proclivities. As I looked into the qualities of Lorna's nature, I saw one of the most open-hearted charts I had ever seen.

In general, the Moon in a birth chart is said to show a person's emotional nature and ability to nurture the self and others. Jupiter brings abundance, while Pluto brings intensity. Pluto can also produce a fixative sort of vibration, causing obsessions over certain things. And thus, we could say that Lorna, having all three of these planets combined, is able to express the following natural temperament:

Abundant, Intense and Fixative Caretaking

The fact that this girl had all three of these planets at the exact same spot in the chart was fascinating and very rare. I excitedly told her father, *" Lorna must be a very giving child!"*

I opened up my *Ephemeris* to see if I could look into the recent past and locate a time period when the *"Intensely Abundant Caretaker "* in Lorna had been activated by the moving planets. I quickly found some appropriate dates.

" We are in luck. This intensely giving part of Lorna was opened up and alivened just two weeks ago on Easter day! Was she doing anything on Easter that might have shown us that her soul really is exceptionally giving?"

Without missing a beat, Lorna's father lit up and told me what had come of this intensely giving energy.

" I can't believe you can see that in the chart! This Easter, Lorna collected a whole basket of plastic eggs filled with candy. The neighbors had scattered them all over the front yard. Lorna wasn't so much interested in eating her candy. Instead, she poured all of her candy into a fishing net, which she then tied to her pink scooter. She told me that she had decided to be the " Easter Man, " her mission in life being to give her candy to everyone in the whole neighborhood. She proceeded to visit every house in the neighborhood, giving away all of her candy!"

Need I say more?

Yellowstone

One of my favorite uses of Astrology is to help couples and families strategically plan and time travel. A quick study of the charts can ensure that family trips fall upon the most happy of times. There is nothing more frustrating than taking the time off of work for an exciting getaway, only to become deathly ill or thwarted in some other fashion.

Often times, clients will come into my office having already planned a long trip, and then ask me about the upcoming astrological weather during this time period. A certain young couple asked me to look into their upcoming road trip through Montana. Since they had already planned the dates, my intent in looking was mainly to see what kinds of emotional weather would be in the Montana air.

I noticed a very concrete blockage on the third to the last day of the upcoming lovers' getaway. While I did not want to ruin their upcoming plans, I also did not want to be caught *not* doing my job, so I mentioned what I had seen.

I began with all of the positive energies that would be assisting the two young lovers on their vacation and then began to provide some options to deal with any blockages.

" *The beginning part of your trip looks phenomenal! If you want to go out and do any sight-seeing, the first part of your trip will be perfect for this! I do see that the third to the last day of the trip might however pose some blockages to the two of you. In fact, you might get thwarted in a very real way. If this happens, there are of course many ways to deal with it. One way is to try to avoid it, another is to try to overcome the adversary. At times, the best approach might be to laugh it off or enjoy the uncanny accuracy of Astrology."*

While I do not like to deliver such news, I know that at times such candor is the most helpful thing of all. The next time I saw these two clients, they spilled the beans. It turns out that they had a wonderful trip. Having forgotten about my prediction, the couple said that they remembered exactly what I had said when they got thwarted in every way, on the third to last day of their trip. On this fateful day, they had encountered a bit of snow while coming through Montana into Wyoming.

The snow was fairly light, so they continued on to their hotel. When they arrived in their cozy room, they noticed that the heater was broken. After going to the front desk to ask for a different room, the couple took off in the car to drive into Yellowstone. In fact, this was the goal of their whole trip, to see the inside of Yellowstone National Park!

As they climbed into the car and started driving, the two lovebirds quickly learned of the constraints of Saturn. When they drove up to Yellowstone, their eyes fell upon the front gates. They noticed a big truck sitting in front of the gates and two men walking the two halves of the gate to the middle, in order to lock up the park. It was at this moment that the couple realized they were witnessing the seasonal closure of Yellowstone National Park. They had driven all this way, only to be entirely thwarted at the gates of their destination.

The young couple said that they enjoyed the magic of this correct prediction, as it had allowed them the ability to laugh off this otherwise disappointing moment. I assured them that Saturn, while cold and distant, does in fact have a sense of humor.

Aunt Kathy

I am often asked, " *How did you figure out that you were psychic?"*

One of my favorite yet most horrifying moments of psychic discovery happened in a very pertinent setting; a *Paranormal Psychology* class at the local University. Years ago, a good friend was taking the class and invited me to come speak to her class about Astrology. Or so I thought.

I prepared some notes about what I wanted to discuss and rode the light rail train downtown to campus. Upon arrival, I entered a large lecture hall filled with Psychology students of all varieties. Slunched over to the right was sporty-psychology guy, who sat looking halfway interested with his hat backwards, waiting for something to perk him out of his apathetic haze.

Before the professor started class, my friend pulled me out into the hall. She wanted to alert me to the fact that her professor was a " total skeptic, " and that she knew I would " wow " him. I was very eager to share my knowledge of Astrology with both apathetic sporty-guy and skeptical-professor man.

The class began with logistical considerations such as future due dates and the topics that would be covered on the upcoming midterm. As the professor finished up, he began to introduce me as the guest speaker. When I heard the introduction, I nearly blew an internal gasket. My friend had told the professor (and the entire class) that I was a bonified psychic! I, on the other hand, had innocently prepared a lecture on Astrology.

As I poised myself and begin talking about Astrology, three hands shot up in the room. I couldn't help but take the questions and soon realized that I had ended up in a *psychic testing zone* of epic proportions. I answered the first two questions, which were both about *spirit guides*. While this topic is interesting, describing someone's spirit guide will never convince a skeptic that such entities exist. In fact, topics such as these enter into the *woo-woo* category, and thus tend to trigger skeptical vibes. Moreover, the existence of a spirit guide will most likely never be scientifically provable.

I called on the third hand, held up by a portly woman sitting to the far right of the lecture hall. Wearing a bright red shirt and a mom haircut, she asked me a more specific question; " *Can you tell me anything about my mom?*"

It turned out that her mom had passed. I had given her a few tidbits of information when a very strong psychic message intruded into my mind's eye. The voice in my head repeated over and over, " *Aunt Kathy, Aunt Kathy, Aunt Kathy.* " The source of this seemingly nonsensical information was relentless.

I finally ask the woman if she had an "Aunt Kathy." She looked at me with wide eyes and said, " *I don't have an Aunt Kathy.*"

My heart skipped a beat and I felt like I might die of embarrassment. I instantly thought, "*Oh my god, I knew it. I surely am not psychic. I am making this all up!*"

Then I heard this same woman shyly perk up again, "*I do however have a very good family friend that we call Aunt Kathy.*"

Another message popped into my mind. "*She is going to be okay. Aunt Kathy is going to be okay.*" Not knowing what else to do, I went ahead and relayed the message, as a very interested class full of students watched on.

The woman burst into tears of joy.

To this day, I still have no idea why Aunt Kathy needed to be okay in the first place, but I am happy that she is. I am even happier that I survived this experience psychically unscathed!

Diversity Training

One day, I received a interesting call. As I answered the phone, a timid yet determined voice said,

"Hi my name is Lea and, umm, I need your help."

As I talked with Lea, I learned that she had seen me lecture in her college class and had called me soon after.

Now it could be said that at certain times in life, there are problems that defy conventional treatment. Lea didn't mention anything of the sort at first, but as I sat down with my colored pencils and ruler, her situation began to emerge before my eyes. I observed a specific planetary pattern, which seemed to indicate that she had been suffering through a rather odd time in her life.

Mercury is the planet which brings communication of all kinds. The energy is chatty, talkative, and wants to connect mentally and verbally. In Lea's chart, the planet of Mercury was in a rather challenging position. The more diffuse and confusing planet of Neptune was touching this girl's Mercury at the time of her birth. When Mercury and Neptune come together in a chart, there can be feelings of confusion in regards to the mind. In fact, it can be quite challenging to discern what is real and what is not when this configuration is present.

As I examined the chart, I noticed that Mercury and Neptune were sitting together in Lea's house of "friendship." This part of her soul was being highlighted in a very intense way at the time of the reading, and thus I knew that there would currently be some sort of activity in this area of her life.

Lea arrived for her reading and looked rather normal. She had long red hair and might have been the type to go to renaissance festivals, which would fit with the fact that her mind tends towards illusion-based thinking.

I began with the basic parts of the chart, spending some time getting to know Lea in reference to her larger personality. When I finally began to talk about her special Neptune/Mercury pile-up, her eyes lit up immediately.

You see, Astrology is the study of all parts of the soul, as well as the timing of the events and experiences that might happen upon it. In the case of Lea, the confusing struggle with friends was occurring at the time she came to get her reading. The situation was serious and Lea's soul was being deeply affected by it. I explained the mixing of the energies the best way that I could.

" *It looks like you might be dealing with some very interesting experiences right now in regards to friendships. Perhaps you have some new friendships right now that are very intense. They may in some way be challenging your way of thinking even. The topics or things they talk about make you wonder what is real and what is not. In a very deep way.*"

Lea voraciously told me what was happening. Up until this point in the reading, she had been very quiet, and now she began to talk fast and furiously about the real reason she had come to see me.

As Lea told me her story, my belief in Astrology grew even deeper.

" *Oh my goodness, I can't believe you can see that in my chart! A while ago, I met these three friends who all think that they are aliens. And I mean that they really think they are from another galaxy! I think that they might really not be human. It is freaking me out! They even tell me details of the galaxies they have come from. I don't know what to do.*"

At times, it is quite surprising just how accurate the astrological chart can be! At other times, it is even more surprising that the universe can come up with circumstances that are so entirely fitting to what is shown in the chart, even when the energies seem altogether bizarre. It could be said that *bizarre astrological energies bring about one-of-a-kind circumstances.*

Astrologers are often asked to help a person who has happened upon unusual circumstances, as these are the kinds of situations that can defy conventional treatment. In the case of this confused and scared young woman, we discussed the societal importance that has been placed on knowing "what is real and what is not. " We also discussed some helpful techniques for living through a time period when reality might not be the overarching theme.

As we wrapped up our long and interesting conversation about aliens, I opened up my planetary book of tables and flipped to the page for that day. I wanted to give the client one final nugget of helpful information before I sent her on her way. I found the date that the current planetary influence would be leaving the young woman's alien-friend configuration.

"The confusing scary energies will be gone for good after January of 2003. Until then, settle in for the ride and take into account all of the things we have discussed here."

The young client left, still feeling a bit confused but no longer afraid. Astrology had been able to give some reality to this otherwise unreal seeming situation.

The Cornucopia

Expecting parents often have a variety of concerns, such as whether or not the baby will be healthy or they will have enough resources to take care of their tiny addition. I remember a certain client by the name of Frederick who was soon to have his first child. As I began to examine his chart, he expressed his concerns about the upcoming year.

As I looked into the months following the arrival of the baby, I noticed a very potent energy. Frederick actually had a very abundant time period approaching! I relayed the news to him, saying,

" *You know Frederick, if you are worried about not having enough resources to take care of the new baby, you can stop now. It looks like the few months after the baby's birth will be filled with abundance. And when I say abundance, I mean a lot of it! In fact, you may get so much help coming that you get a bit overwhelmed.*"

The planet of Jupiter and the planet of Venus were connected in Frederick's chart. Venus tends to rule love and gift-giving, and can be said to bring about happiness through sweetness and connection. Jupiter can amplify anything it touches in a chart, often in a very positive way. Needless to say, when Jupiter and Venus are touching in a person's birth chart, there are times when sweet things come in floods.

I mentioned to Frederick that the only problem with his upcoming luck was that there just might be too much of it! As we finished up the reading and Frederick was set to go on his way, he expressed his hope that my *abundance prediction* would in fact come true. He wanted to be able to relax and enjoy the new baby. I assured Frederick that he would have more than enough resources at his disposal.

Frederick and his wife had a precious baby boy and soon after the gifts started flooding in!

Packages showed up in the mail full of baby toys, clothes, trinkets, diapers, etc. In fact, so much stuff had arrived at the house that Frederick made a point to call me.

" *You were absolutely right! There are so many packages coming in that I can't even keep up. In fact, some of this stuff is made in a way that I can't even figure out how to use it! I now have Boppies and Burpies, and a hundred blue onesies. The packages just keep arriving on my doorstep!"*

It is times like this that the universe seems to have a sense of humor. Perhaps it is possible to have *too much of a good thing*, as they say.

In this case, Frederick said that he was rather enjoying the *love flood* but he was not looking forward to the large pile of thank you notes that he would soon be writing. As we were about to hang up the phone, Frederick asked me one last question, " *So riddle me this.*

Can Astrology tell me how to write a thank you note for something if I can't even figure out what it is!?"

And to this I responded, " *Not unless we know its birth time!"*

The Dotted Line

I knew who he was the exact moment I saw him. He was talking excitedly about his time in Vietnam, and he spoke with a vernacular that sounded oddly like a mix between a surfer and a stagehand. I found him both mesmerizing and hilarious at the same time. I had suspected that something like this would be happening soon, as every time an important person enters my life, I feel an immense sense of *knowing*. As an astrologer looking at my own astrological chart, I could see that my soul was soon to be entering a time of great change and excitement in relation to child rearing. I was sure I might soon have a baby!

At the time I was resistant to the idea, but just as my chart had revealed, there appeared future-daddy Vietnam stagehand-guy. This meeting marked the beginning of a wild ride. Have I mentioned that said future-daddy never was in Vietnam? I learned this fact as we chatted that night, half-knowingly beginning a beautiful friendship.

I felt very deeply that this man and I would be having a baby in December of the following year, so I promptly told him so; on our first date.

People often ask me why on earth I would have said this so soon. This is where the life of an astrologer becomes quite interesting, in a bizarre and challenging way. In my psychic and internal sensors, I felt that this man was absolutely the father of my future child. Yet in our astrological charts, it appeared that in the three months following our meeting, we would certainly *not* get along. In fact, it looked like we might just downright hate each other.

Luckily, there was hope. In the field of Astrology, there is a wonderful technique that allows an astrologer to analyze the future relationship of two individuals. More precisely, an astrologer can see how the two energy fields will mix, and whether or not the two people will meld into a partnership that is easy to handle. The composite chart of my future baby's Dad and I promised great amounts of creative energy, wonderful communication, and open hearts. As in, said daddy-to-be and I would not meld into cold, cranky parents.

So there I sat at my desk, wondering how I might handle this oddly sticky situation. I could see that this man and I could have a great future, raising a child in a creative and joyful way. But we also happened to have met at a time during which the planets were entirely unforgiving for either of our astrological charts. I didn't mind this so much, as I have watched hard astrological weathers pass for years and can see when the hard times will end. I was more concerned that he and I could walk through the weather gracefully, and meld into a possible *parental friendship of love.*

And so I thought. Then I thought some more. I considered many options of how to proceed.

Then it dawned on me! I could devise a *future hard times coalition contract*. I thought, maybe we could both just agree to keep trying until the energies had passed.

It was in this moment that I decided to *try out* the *future hard times coalition contract* in order to remedy future struggles before they might happen. On our first "future parenting date," I asked him to sign the contact. As he tells the story now, he at the time thought I was nuts "in the best sort of way."

The three month struggle was formidable. It went something like this: fourteen plans broken, a few verbal altercations, three thousand text messages, a set of keys thrown, and a yelling match on a speedboat on the Columbia River. It was at this point that preordained-daddy told me that he couldn't take me seriously until I was 30 years old and I told him to wait until I was 40 years old to speak to me again.

Needless to say, the contract was necessary!

Our daughter will soon be entering kindergarten and we routinely birth creative projects together, collaborating on design and artistic concepts for the books that we publish through the Moira Press. We have melded into a very loving and positive parental unit, approaching every struggle with an unspoken *future hard times coalition contract*.

I'm Your Venus!

A few years after giving birth to my daughter, I decided that I was ready to branch out and find a nice *lady friend*. At the time, my days were most often spent with my daughter and my now best friend, who also happens to be her Dad. My daughter's father and I continue to have a great family-friendship to this very day, but the time had come for me to manifest some romance.

Anyone who has known me for any length of time can attest to the fact that I am energetically sensitive to an extreme degree. As a bonified psychic, this condition seems to come with the territory. For any woman, the experience of motherhood is one that seems to be accompanied by a variety of emotions, and as could be expected, having a baby had made my sensitivity even more acute. This was partially true on account of being responsible for a set of tiny little emotions, and partly because having a child makes integration with new people into a sport all its own. Often times, a child's need to cry and carry on produces negative emotions in the adults who are in close vicinity, and a *sensitive-mama* can have a hard time navigating between such differing emotional needs.

When my daughter was almost two years old, I finally felt like I had become wise to the world of motherhood. The next thing to attend to was mama's emotional need for a romantic partnership. As is true of children and their mothers, the need for happiness goes both ways. As in, if mama is not happy, then her babies can not quite be truly content either.

Having studied and practiced *Relationship Astrology* for many years, I felt confident that I would be able to manifest a good situation for the whole family. One of the most practical uses of Astrology is to calculate the mutual *vibe* that will be created when two people "*Energy Love Mingle.*"

For an energetically sensitive person, the *vibe* in a love relationship is very, very important. In the most simple terms, it could be said that *sensitive people need highly encouraging vibes.*

Most people seem to discuss partnership in terms of realistic principles such as long-term financial success, religious compatibility, physical needs, common values and interests, etc. For an energetically sensitive person, these factors seem to be much less important than the vibration that is created between two people in a love relationship.

As a mother, I knew that I had to proceed in a delicate fashion, as the introduction of any new relationship into a family system has the potential to alter the entire dynamic. My daughter's Dad and I had already been privy to more than a few new friendship energies during our long-term *Parenting Love Mingle.*

On account of the delicate nature of the current emotional situation, I decided that I needed some assistance from the divine and upper realms.

As mentioned, the *composite chart* is an astrological chart that is calculated for the vibrational mixing of two individuals. In other words, the composite chart will show how two people will *vibe* together, and what kinds of emotions will be created over the long term.

Primed and ready for romance, I sat down and began to do some calculations. I thought long and hard, envisioning the most optimal composite chart for my sensitive nature. I told the universe that I was ready for "the one," meaning that this future lady-lover must also merge well with my daughter and her father. I made a promise to myself to not even go on a date with any lady until I had checked the composite charts for all members of my family. If one of these combinations did not indicate a brighter future, I would " jump ship " right then and there.

The fated calculation day came and went.

I continued with life as normal, doing Astrology readings and translating ancient Greek texts in the privacy of my tiny basement office.

Then something happened that changed my whole life.

I received an email from a former Astrology client. Now this wasn't just any client, but a girl that I had originally met through playing music. In fact, we had met years earlier at the Portland-based *Rock n' Roll Camp for Girls*, where she worked as a volunteer guitar instructor and I taught drums to young rockers. This particular lady had later been my Astrology client, but the vibration underneath was more of an " acquaintance-turned-friend. " I remember secretly wishing that we could just take our relationship into the official *friend zone*.

Now it must be understood that I get emails from clients all the time. This was nothing new. But on this particular day, the email surprised me. This "client" had written to me about a dream! She mentioned that the message in the dream was so strong that she could not resist writing me, even though such an email could be considered in professional terms to be "inappropriate."

I got that feeling of *knowing* in my gut. I knew that this somehow was connected to my love calculations. I raced to my reading table and opened up my *Ephemeris*. I speedily calculated our combined energies.

There it was! The *exact* composite chart that I had asked for from the upper realms!

I had known this girl for almost eight years! And just one week after I had asked for a lady-friend, she had seen us coming together as *friends* in her dream.

As I had promised myself, I checked out the manner in which this lady would merge with the rest of the family, and I saw only good possibilities! So we went on a date. We are still together to this day and have melded into all kinds of good vibrations.

While this story is personal, I tell it as a testament to the ability of people to manifest happiness through the use of Astrology. Vibrations can in fact be calculated and a relationship that is vibrationally supportive is much, much easier to handle than the alternative. In other words, some people feel very good around one another, naturally. For others, getting along can be quite difficult.

I often wonder why someone has not yet started an online dating service that matches people up according to their astrological charts. Now this would be a highly beneficial and positive use of Astrology!

Heat Wave

Every so often, I am introduced to a problem that even doctors cannot figure out. While I do not claim to be able to diagnose and treat medical disorders per se, it could be said that Astrology can be quite helpful and accurate in regards to the timing of physical ailments. This use of Astrology generally functions in correlation with the idea that germs do indeed exist around us, but we become sick when we are emotionally or energetically depleted in some manner.

I remember a very sensitive client who was referred to me through a close friend. It seemed as if Trula's physical health was very much connected with her emotional state. The manifestation of her stress came in the form of a very odd syndrome that could not be explained; burning armpits. When I say *burning* here, I mean that she experienced such intense discomfort that she could not function normally. It was very painful to wear clothes over such fiery pockets, and Trula was becoming desperate.

I examined the chart and noticed something very striking in the section related to health problems. The planet of Mars was sitting in the sign of Cancer exactly on top of the *North Node of the Moon*. In medical Astrology, it is often said that any planet which is on top of to the *North Node* is amplified greatly. In other words, the *North Node* can bring in an excess of energy, which can at times cause intense and noticeable health problems.

In medical Astrology, the sign in which a planet is sitting shows the part of the body in which the energy expresses itself. The planet of Mars brings in *heat*. Most simply, the equation appeared as follows:

Mars = Hot
North Node = Amplification
Cancer = Armpits

Mars + North Node in Cancer =
An amplification of heat in the armpits.

I pulled out my *Ephemeris* and began to look back in time. I asked Trula if her armpits had been on fire two weeks earlier. She looked a bit surprised but said yes! I looked back a bit further in order to find another time period of inflammation and armpit burning. Success!

After timing three episodes of past flare-ups, I wrote down a few future dates. I told Trula,

" Please watch these dates in the future as your armpit-fire might in fact flare up. If this does occur, it will be important to remember that your body tends to get more heated up than others. I recommend all sorts of cooling methods, such as sucking on ice, not wearing excessively hot clothes, or taking cold showers. Definitely, whatever you do, avoid Cayenne supplements and hot food on these days, as they can heat up the stomach and make the problem worse."

I never did hear from Trula again, yet I did run into her boyfriend many years later in a Portland dive bar. He expressed his profound state of *astrological awe* over the fact that I had predicted several correct dates for Trula's " burning armpit " flare ups. He also mentioned that Trula had successfully figured out how to control the problem!

The Red Shirt

Last night over dinner, an astrological colleague of mine asked me a probing question. He said, " *If you are in fact psychic, why do you not just do psychic readings? Why do you even bother to use the astrological chart?"*

The answer to this question is that the astrological chart is useful for certain questions, while psychic information attends to different kinds of answers. As Judith states in the *Introduction,* Astrology is not of itself a psychic science, although one can opt to use the birth chart as a means for observing the needs and urges of the soul and psyche. For instance, the astrological chart can indicate the manner in which a client's current situation fits in with the entirety of their life path. The chart is very good at timing events, the end of hard times, and the beginning of better *emotional weather.*

As astrologers, we know that the chart of the planetary positions at birth indicates the lifelong energetic tendencies of an individual. The emissions from the moving planets then come in and out of the *natally-determined* energy field, allowing that same individual to breath and grow as the years progress. For instance, if a parent were to come into my office to have a look at their child's chart in reference to a certain " problem behavior, " the birth chart of that child would show whether or not the behaviors are just a phase, or are tendencies that will exist for the entirety of the life.

Psychic information, in my case, is knowledge that I am able to obtain from the *divine and upper realms*. For instance, I might consult with my guides as to the best manner in which to deal with an ongoing problem that is indicated in the chart. As I say on my radio show, " *May we honor and revere the fated fates and turn everything else into the greatest greats.* " The chart will show us the " fated fates, " while psychic information attends to the "greatest greats."

Moreover, there are times when the upper and divine realms have something quite important to say about certain questions.

I will never forget Eleana, as our reading taught me an important lesson about this very matter.

Eleana was an actress turned metal recycler, and at the time of her reading was in the process of looking for love. I talked a bit about the astrological timing of her " love search, " but as the reading progressed, I felt the psychic images come streaming into my consciousness, through the air to the front and right side of my face.

There I saw them; two shirts.

My psychic sensors had landed on two polo shirts floating in the air! Then all of a sudden one of the shirts showed itself to be red, while the other was emerging to be distinctly red and white.

Needless to say, psychic images such as these can be quite elusive to the psychic herself! Over the years, I have learned the very important lesson of not *interpreting* these pictures, as I am never sure what the pictures mean. I have discovered however that the client almost always knows the exact meaning of the image!

In this case, I described the floating polo shirts to Eleana, and her eyes turned into huge saucers of surprise. She couldn't believe the accuracy of the message. It turns out that she had just started dating two guys that she had met through the internet. On their first date, both men had worn polo shirts; one was red and the other was red and white. Eleana was trying to choose between these two men.

After getting confirmation that the image was pertinent, the picture of the red shirt dissolved, while the red and white polo shirt remained hanging in the air like a persistent omen. No matter which way Eleana and I discussed her love life, the red and white polo shirt kept popping up.

This is exactly the kind of information that the astrological chart will *not* tell us. The chart did in fact show that Eleana was looking for love and that she might be confused in her search. Yet in this case, the divine and upper realms stepped in to give her some extra information and guidance!

Manifest Destiny

People often ask me how I know a thought is a " psychic message," as opposed to a "normal thought." While the answer to this question is not all that simple, this story describes the experience perfectly!

I will never forget a client from many years ago named Deonna. On the day of her reading, Deonna pleasantly surprised me by being a butch dyke. Over the phone, Deonna's name had not conjured up images of female masculinity, yet in person it was quite clear that Deonna was the strong silent type. She said very little, yet her vibe was striking and best described as " pure-hearted farm girl meets intense bad boy."

I directed Deonna to take a seat in my tiny Portland garage-office. As I pressed "record" on the tape player, I focused on the layout of Deonna's chart. Per normal protocol, I started with an explanation of some of the basic attributes of Deonna's Sun, Moon, and Rising signs.

As the clock ticked gently in the background, Deonna's reading progressed uneventfully. Then all of a sudden, something very interesting happened! A picture of a religious-looking Cross formed clearly in my psychic mind.

Being a baby astrologer and budding psychic at the time, I was reluctant to describe what I was seeing to the intensely quiet butch dyke sitting in front of me. I instead went on with my explanation of her chart, but no matter how hard I tried to ignore it, my mind wandered back to the image. Again and again I saw the large Cross, just sitting there in space, waiting for me to describe what I was seeing to Deonna.

As I further perused the details of Deonna's chart, I noticed that it did in fact seem to support what I had seen in my psychic vision. I thought to myself, "*This girl could be an amazing minister. Wow, this chart is truly divine and spiritually driven. Wow.*"

Now remember, Deonna had shown up in my office with short spiky hair, huge arm muscles, a plaid shirt, and goth boots. This situation perfectly illustrates one of those times when a psychic message floods in, but the information from the unseen realm doesn't make much sense in the real world.

As in, a silent butch bad *boi* does not a minister make.

Needless to say, before a message is confirmed to be true, it can make the psychic receiver feel a bit nutty. The moment that a pressing feeling like this gets real world confirmation is the point at which the *psycho feeling* retroactively turns into a *psychic feeling*.

Now back to Deonna. As the reading continued, there it came again, the large and detailed image of a Cross. This time, the picture was accompanied by an urgent feeling that I simply *must* tell Deonna what I was seeing. A voice in my head was now repeating,

"Religion. Religion. Religion. Religion."

I looked at Deonna and said, "*You know, I have never had a message like this before, so it must be very specific to you. No matter what I do, I cannot shake the feeling that you are supposed to be a minister! In fact, I keep seeing an intricate cross in my mind's eye.*"

It was at this point that Deonna began to tear up. I popped up to grab the tissue box but Deonna stopped me with her boxy butch hand and said, "*Thank you so much!*"

As she wiped the tears from her eyes, Deonna heartily rolled up the sleeve of her plaid flannel shirt in order to expose a huge tattoo of an intricate and shining Cross! It turns out that Deonna had always and forever wanted to be a youth minister but had been kicked out of her local church for being gay.

Needless to say, it must have been the right time for a new beginning!

"For several hundred years there has been a bias in western education against the intuitive approach in medicine and science. Intuition, imagination and instinct are relegated to art or religion. There it is permissible to use such faculties. While one can appreciate the need for objective and analytical study, the use of these methods alone, as if they were the only true measures of reality, in and of itself, is an inherently sick and flawed condition. It skews the human organism by rendering obsolete skills and faculties it has always relied upon to contend with environmental and internal stress."

Matthew Wood, Herbalist, author
The Practice of Western Herbalism[5]

---

[5] quote from page 14

Books By Judith Hill

The Astrological Body Types (revised and expanded), Stellium Press, 1997 (available through Book People, A.F.A., Inc.) Note: Russian and Lettish language editions available through Astroinformservis, Latvia. Second revision 2012

The Part of Fortune in Astrology, Stellium Press, 1998, 2010

Vocational Astrology: A Complete Handbook of Western Astrological Career Selection and Guidance Techniques, A.F.A. Inc., 1999

The Mars-Redhead Files, Stellium Press, 2000 (compendium of published astro-genetic research by Hill and Hill-Thompson)

Astroseismology: Earthquakes and Astrology, Stellium Press, 2000 (Compendium of published research by Hill and Hill-Polit)

Medical Astrology: A Guide to Planetary Pathology, Stellium Press, 2005

Mrs. Winkler's Cure: Stellium Press, 2010 (original fairy tales published under pen name Julia Holly).

The Lunar Nodes: Your Key to Excellent Chart Interpretation, Stellium Press, 2010.

Eclipses and You (edited by Tony Howard), Stellium Press, 2013

Journal Articles by Judith Hill

"The Mars-Redhead Link," Judith A. Hill & Jacalyn Thompson, NCGR Journal, Winter 88-89 (first published by *Above & Below* (Canada); *Linguace Astrale* (Italy); *AA Journal* (Great Britain); *FAA Journal* (Australia)

"The Mars-Redhead Link II: Mars Distribution Patterns in Redhead Populations," *Borderlands Research Sciences Foundation Journal*, Vol. L1, No. 1 (Part 1) and Vol. L1, No 2 (Part 2)

"Commentary on the John Addey Redhead Data," *NCGR Journal*, Winter 88-89 "Redheads and Mars," *The Mountain Astrologer*, May 1996

"Correlation of Earthquakes with Planetary Placement: The Regional Factor," Judith A. Hill & Mark Polit *NCGR Journal*, 5 (1), 1987.

"The Regional Factor in Planetary-Seismic Correlation", *Borderlands Research Sciences Foundation Journal*, Vol.L1, Number 3, 1995 (reprint courtesy of American Astrology)

"American Redhead's Project Replication", *Correlation*, Volume 13, No 2, Winter 94-95

"Octaves of Time," *Borderlands Research Journal*, Vol. L1, Number 4, Fourth Quarter, 1995

"Gemstones, Antidotes for Planetary Weaknesses," *ISIS Journal*, 1994

"Medical Astrology," *Borderlands Research Journal*, Vol. L11, Number 1, First Quarter, 1996

"Astrological Heredity," *Borderlands Research Journal*, 1996

"The Electional and Horary Branches," *Sufism, IAS*, Vol. 1, No 1

"Astrology: A Philosophy of Time and Space," *Sufism, IAS*, Vol. 1, No 1

"Natal Astrology," *Sufism, IAS*, Vol. 1, No 3

"An Overview of Medical Astrology," *Sufism, IAS*, Vol. 1, No 4

"Predictive Astrology in Theory and Practice," *Sufism, IAS*, Vol. 11, No 1

"Esoteric Astrology," *Sufism, IAS*, Vol. 11, No 2, 3

"Mundane Astrology," *Sufism, IAS*, Vol. 11, No 4

"Vocational Astrology," *Sufism, IAS*, Parts 1 and 2, Vol. 111, No 1, 2

"Astro-Psychology," *Sufism, IAS*, Vol. 111, No 3, 4

"The Planetary Time Clocks," *Sufism, IAS*, Vol. 4, No. 1, 2, 3, 4

"Astrophysiognomy," *Sufism, IAS*, Vol. 4, No 1, 2

"Spiritual Signposts in the Birth Map," *Sufism, IAS*, Vol. 5, No 2,3

"The Philosophical Questions Most Frequently Asked of the Astrology," *Sufism, IAS*, Vol. 5, No 4, Vol. 6, No 12

"Music and the Ear of the Beholder," *Sufism, IAS*, 1999

"The Astrology of Diabetes," *Dell Horoscope*, October 2003

"A Life Time of Astrology," published interview with Judith Hill by Tony Howard, *The Mountain Astrologer Magazine*, Nov-Dec, 2010

Books by Andrea L. Gehrz

Porphyry of Tyre, *An Introduction to the Tetrabiblios of Ptolemy,* Translated by Andrea L. Gehrz. Portland, Oregon, The Moira Press, 2010

Vettius Valens of Antioch, *Anthology: Book One*, Translated by Andrea L. Gehrz. Portland, Oregon, The Moira Press, 2011

Astrological Remediation: A Guide for the Modern Practitioner, Andrea L. Gehrz. Portland, Oregon, The Moira Press, 2012

Illustrations

Linoleum cut, by Robert Hill, 1957 with restorative changes by J. Hill, 2012

Planetary rulers of the seven days of the week, French, from Le Petit Albert's Secretes Merveilleux de la Magie, Cologne, 1722

page 22: Magellan's ship Victoria, first vessel to circumnavigate the globe in 1522, skippered by Juan Sebastian del Cano 16th century engraving.

page 31: The Sun as the primary moveable star, from Italian card deck, fifteenth century

page 90: Charles and Robert Montgolfier's first ascent in a manned balloon, Paris, Dec 1783

page 139: Arabic astrologer constructing a celestial globe from Alboul Hassan Ali's Praeclarissimus in Juditijs Astroum, Venice 1519

page 193: Reproduction of Tycho Brahe's equatorial armillary sphere by Levin Hulsi, Nuremberg, 1598

page 200: Allegory of the month of April riding in upon Taurus, English calendar, 1866

Back Cover: Portrait of William Lilly, one of the most famous Renaissance astrologers. Author of *Christian Astrology* who predicted the great fire of London in September of 1666.

About Judith Hill

Judith Hill is a life time, second generational astrologer and award winning author. She has performed over 9000 in depth personal readings and is proficient in most branches of Classical Western Astrology including: Vocation, Location, Medical, Natal, Transit-Progressed, Spiritual, Comparative Analysis, Electional (selecting dates for important life events); Gem Selection; Fertility Dating and Horary Astrology (the art of answering special questions from exact times). Her consulting experience is vast, having read for men and women of most nations, ages and professions. She is also well versed in the outside subjects of: Herbology, Vedic Astrology, History, Theology, Illustration arts, Sculpture, Music, Metaphysics, Feng Shui, Phrenology, Physiognomy, Psychology, Palmistry, Graphology and Anthropology.

Her first paid astrological reading was at the age of fourteen, following a four year intensive training with a skilled relative. She has been reading charts for every possible type of person ever since!

Hill successfully matched five charts to five biographies in an NCGR sponsored skeptics' challenge in 1989. Judith was awarded the Paul R. Grell "Best Book Award" from American Federation of Astrologers, Inc. for AFA publications, 1999 for *Vocational Astrology*.

She is the author of many other books including the now classic *Astrological Body Types*. Her additional titles include *The Part of Fortune in Astrology; Medical Astrology: A Guide to Planetary Pathology; The Lunar Nodes: Your Key to Excellent Chart Reading; Vocational Astrology*; and two acclaimed research compendiums: *The Mars-Redhead Files*; and *Astroseismology*. Several of Hill's books are listed as "top ten" books by genre with "The Astrology Center of America." Selected books and articles have been translated into Italian, Russian and Lettish.

Hill was a writer for four years for the *IAS*. Her articles were historic as a probable first in-depth scholastic quarterly on Astrology outside of the astrological press.

Judith served as the "Educational Director" for the San Francisco *National Council for Geocosmic Research (NCGR)* and as a faculty member for *The Institute of Stellar Influence Studies*.

Radio appearances have included interviews on: KCBS, KPFA, KBOO, *The Laura Lee Show*, *The Mitch Rabin Show*; The NYC based *"Job 1" Show* and Andrea L. Gehrz's *The Astrological Detective*.

Judith has made significant contributions to the scientific and statistical research of Astrology. She completed reports in both astro-genetics and astro-seismology. Her findings have been included in numerous journals such as:

Borderland Sciences Research Foundation Journal;
NCGR Journal; Correlations (UK); The Mountain Astrologer;
Dell Horoscope; Above and Below; Linguace Astrale, and others.

Ms. Hill Founded "The Redheads Research Project" - an international ten year statistical analysis of Astrology and genetics; resulting in an international publication with co researcher Jacalyn Thompson. Hill and Thompson's breakthrough research in astro-genetics was featured on TV's *Strange Universe*. Her breakthrough astro-seismological research work, conducted in partnership with co-researcher Mark Polit, received a research grant from the renowned physicist Arthur Young and his *Institute for the Study of Consciousness* in Berkeley, California. Judith received the degree of Chartered Herbalist from *The Dominion College of Herbal Sciences*.

She founded Stellium Press, a publishing house dedicated to fine astrological, whimsical and spiritual books (accepts no manuscripts).

Speaking Engagements: Plant Medicine Conference; The International Association of Sufism; The Theosophical Society; The Daughters of the American Revolution; Sacred Places Conference; The Oregon Astrological Association, The Washington State Astrological Association; The National Council for Geocosmic Research; The Institute for the Study of Consciousness; The American Federation of Astrologers, Inc.

About Andrea L. Gehrz

Andrea Gehrz currently lives and practices Astrology in Portland, Oregon. She grew up in St. Paul, Minnesota and went on to graduate *Summa cum Laude* from the University of Minnesota with a Bachelor 's degree in Individualized Studies (B.I.S). Andrea then went on to formally study Sign Language Interpreting at St. Paul Technical College.

After many years in the field of ASL interpreting, Andrea picked up her first Astrology book. Since that time, she has done over 2000 readings for clients, has translated two ancient Greek astrological texts, and has written a book on the manner in which to heal problems in any astrological chart.

Andrea's first translation was an introductory book to Claudius Ptolemy's infamous and historically important text entitled the *Tetrabiblos*. This translation, originally written by Neo-Platonic philosopher Porphyry of Tyre, won an *Independent Book Publishing Award* in the Philosophy & Classics division in 2011. Andrea's second translation also has received acclaim, as it is the first in a nine book Anthology written by the ancient practicing astrologer Vettius Valens.

Andrea has also been a lifelong musician, having toured the country extensively with bands. She started piano lessons at the age of 4, and now incorporates music into her multi-dimensional radio show entitled *The Astrological Detective*. Andrea has played in numerous bands, including *Punky Bruiser* from Minneapolis and the Portland-based two piece drum and cello duo *Discharge Information System*. She currently enjoys playing drums in her two-piece metal/electronic duo entitled *TraumaDom*. Andrea also does side projects, such as playing drums in a cover band of ladies doing *Megadeth* and *Metallica* songs.

After birthing her daughter Angelene, Andrea turned her astrological focus to the art of healing through the use of Astrology. She has designed real-time art therapy projects matched up exactly to the charts of certain clients. Andrea attempts to heal the most challenging of struggles, as she believes the uses of Astrology to be vast and profound. She currently focuses her astrological research into the area of geniuses, children, family systems, ancient Greek translation, and Remediation. She routinely lectures to Astrology groups, college associations, and spiritual centers. She would love to hear from you!

My very own Astral Schematic[6]

as drawn by:

---

[6] *On the following page is a blank astrological chart. Once you know your birth date, time, and location, you can calculate your own chart by use of this template!*

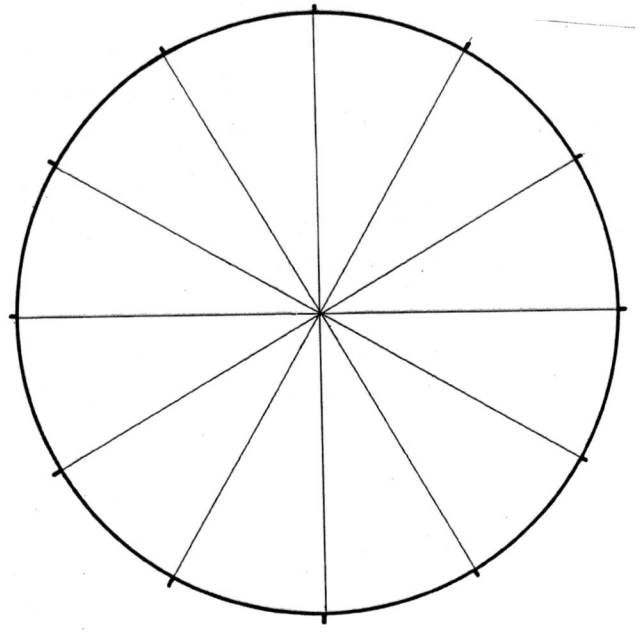

Name:

Birth Date:
Location:
Time:

CPSIA information can be obtained
at www.ICGtesting.com
Printed in the USA
LVOW11s1313110618
580310LV00001B/44/P

9 780982 789339